DUE

J

VANISHED
MESOAMERICAN
CIVILIZATIONS

ERNESTO GONZÁLEZ LICÓN is Professor and Curator at the National Museum of Anthropology in Mexico City. He has conducted archaeological research in various regions of Mexico, including Chiapas, Yucatán, Mexico City, Morelos, and particularly in Oaxaca. From 1987 to 1989 he was the head of the Archaeology Department at the National Museum of Anthropology. From 1989 to 1992 he was the Director of the Oaxaca Regional Center of the National Institute of Anthropology and History, and Director of the Monte Albán Project. His publications include *Los Mayas de la Gruta de Loltún, Yucatán* (1986), *Costumbres funerarias en Monte Albán* (1990), and *La zona oaxaqueña en el Posclásico* (1995).

VANISHED MESOAMERICAN CIVILIZATIONS

The History and Cultures of the Zapotecs and Mixtecs

ERNESTO GONZÁLEZ LICÓN

Appendix: María Luisa Franco Brizuela
Translation: Andrew Ellis
Consultant: Susan Kart, Columbia University

SHARPE REFERENCE
an imprint of M.E. Sharpe, Inc.

SHARPE REFERENCE

Sharpe Reference is an imprint of M.E. Sharpe INC.

M.E. Sharpe INC.
80 Business Park Drive
Armonk, NY 10504

© 2001 M.E. Sharpe INC.
Copyright © 1991
by Editoriale Jaca Book spa, Milano
All rights reserved.

Original title
Tremila anni di civiltà Precolombiana.
Zapotechi e Mixtechi

Library of Congress Cataloging-in-Publication Data

Gonzáles Licón, Ernesto
    [Tremila anni di civiltà precolombiana zapotechi e mixtechi. Italian]
    Vanished Mesoamerican civilizations : the history and cultures of the Zapotecs and
Mixtecs / Ernesto Gonzáles Licón.
        p. cm.
    Includes bibliographical references and index.
    ISBN 0-7656-8035-1 (alk. Paper)
        1. Zapotec Indians—Antiquities. 2. Mixtec—Antiquities. 3. Oaxaca (Mexico)—Antiquities [1.
Zapotec Indians. 2. Mixtec Indians. 3. Indians of Mexico.] I. Title.

F1219.8.Z37 G65162000
972'.7401–dc21   00-055641

Printed and bound in Italy

Translated from Italian by
Andrew Ellis

For M.E. Sharpe INC.
Vice President and Director, Sharpe Reference: Evelyn M. Fazio
Vice President and Production Director: Carmen P. Chetti
Senior Reference Editor: Andrew Gyory
Reference Production Manager: Wendy E. Muto
Cover Design: Lee Goldstein

Contents

Foreword

The archaeological region of Oaxaca presented in this volume is a region of special importance. Situated in the heart of Mesoamerica, Oaxaca underwent influence from the Central Plateau and from the Maya region alike, besides generating rich cultures of its own in the Zapotec and Mixtec legacy, which can be traced back to a very distant past and cover much of the vast territory corresponding to modern-day Oaxaca.

The best-known towns and cities of this fertile archaeological area include Monte Albán, San José Mogote, Yagul, Dainzú, Lambityeco, and Mitla, which thrived in the Central Valleys of Oaxaca and cast their influence over other important Mesoamerican centers. Such was the case with Teotihuacán,[1] the first "metropolis" of central Mexico, where an entire residential quarter has been discovered. The site is thought to have belonged to an artisan community of Oaxaca, given the great quantity of pottery and other related material originating in that region.

Both Zapotec and Mixtec cultures had a distinct impact on Oaxaca. Although their knowledge was basically akin to that of other Mesoamerican peoples, the Zapotecs and Mixtecs created a highly original type of architecture, and a distinct style of sculpture and pottery. Prime examples are the supremely harmonious plaza at Monte Albán, the characteristic Zapotec tombs, and the pottery of the Mixtecs, who also proved themselves accomplished goldsmiths.

The Mixtec codices deserve a special mention as invaluable sources of rites, history, and mythology.

Today we have acquired new insights into the world of these two ancient peoples thanks to the writings of archaeologist Ernesto González Licón, the present Director of the Centro Regional de Oaxaca of the INAH, and previously the curator of the Sala de Oaxaca and the Sub-Director of Archaeology of the Museo Nacional de Antropología, Mexico City.

The volume is complemented by a closing Appendix by María Luisa Franco Brizuela, Director of the Dirección de Restauración del Patrimonio Cultural of the INAH, who, from 1987 to 1988, conducted the restoration of one of the latest archaeological discoveries in the Oaxaca region: the painted tomb at Huijazóo.

In the pages that follow we will examine the historical and ongoing archaeological research that has made it possible to lift the veil which has hidden these two cultures for so many centuries.

EDUARDO MATOS MOCTEZUMA

To Lourdes, my wife;
Without her I would not have been able to write this book.

To all those anonymous people whose devotion and toil
created such extraordinary cities in pre-Hispanic times, and
later brought them to light that we might admire their
glory. Without these souls, this book would never have
been written.

Introduction
The Region of Oaxaca

Introduction

The Region of Oaxaca

Oaxaca, one of the vast cultural areas into which scholars tend to divide Mesoamerica, coincides approximately with today's modern state of Oaxaca. In pre-Columbian times the region was the habitat of important ethnic groups such as the Mixes, the Chatinos, the Chinantecs, and Cuicatecs, but the most prominent groups were the Zapotecs and Mixtecs.

There is a saying that the easiest way to illustrate the extraordinarily rugged geography of Oaxaca is to crumple a piece of paper. This is largely true, but there are also important valleys, such as Nochixtlán Valley in the Mixtec area, and the Valley of Oaxaca in the central area. Vast plains and dense woodlands cover the Isthmus and the area of Tuxtepec, while the Pacific coast is characterized by a narrow stretch of flat land and the sweeping river basin of the Cañada.

From the point of view of cultural development, the valleys played a fundamental role in fostering urban settlements, as they offered fertile land that was very accessible and easy to irrigate. In the region's central plateaus, the Valley of Oaxaca is unusual for both its form and its size, and comprises three smaller valleys, the Etla in the northwest, the Tlacolula in the southeast, and the Zaachila-Zimatlán in the south, crossed by the Atoyac River (which runs from north to south) and its tributaries. This habitat was the site of important towns such as Mitla in the Tlacolula Valley, and Monte Albán, sited on a high ledge 1,300 feet (400 meters) above sea level, overlooking the valley, and 2.5 miles (4 kilometers) as the crow flies from the site of today's town of Oaxaca.

These and many other important pre-Hispanic urban centers caught the attention of travelers and chroniclers of later eras. Their descriptions, and accounts of more recent date, have provided archaeologists with useful bearings for extensive and detailed research campaigns. Excavations have gradually enriched our knowledge of the early inhabitants of Oaxaca and their culture. A great many questions remain unanswered, however. As we shall see, until midway through this century research had focused almost exclusively on the larger archaeological sites in the Valley of Oaxaca, i.e., on Monte Albán and Mitla. It was not until the 1950s that systematic excavations were undertaken in other areas. This explains why our overall knowledge of the Oaxaca region is so incomplete and biased: we have a mine of information on the major sites in the Central Valleys, and yet research into sites in other zones is almost nonexistent or at best fragmentary.

This book aims to provide an overview of the cultural and historical development of the two main ethnic groups that inhabited Oaxaca in pre-Hispanic times—the Zapotecs and the Mixtecs. Other groups will be treated more briefly either because basic information is lacking or because our understanding of them is still largely guesswork. In some cases the first results of investigations are still being developed.

This book gives as complete a picture as possible of current knowledge of pre-Hispanic Oaxaca, and offers the vast audience interested in Mesoamerican cultures a simple and accessible guide to the investigations undertaken in the Oaxaca region over the past 500 years.

1. The State of Oaxaca.

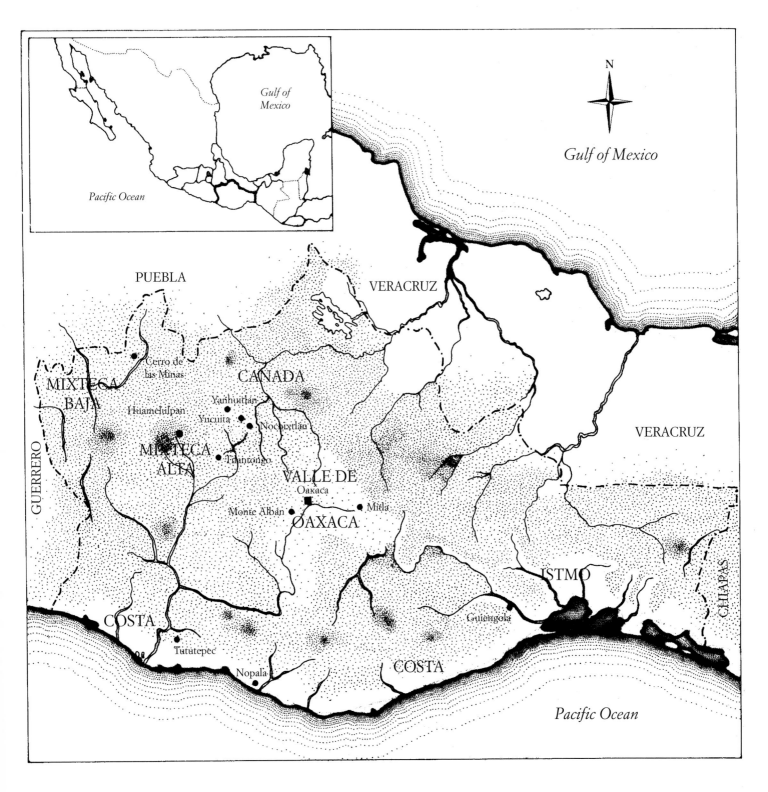

Chapter One
A History of Archaeological Explorations in Oaxaca

Chapter One

A History of Archaeological Explorations in Oaxaca

When he first alighted on the shores of Veracruz in 1519, Hernán Cortés was soon apprised of the existence of a thriving and productive region south of the great Aztec capital of México-Tenochtitlán. A gift of gold pieces from the region in question fired his curiosity, and that same year he dispatched one of his trusted captains, Francisco de Orozco, to Huaxyácac to investigate the origin of the objects and to ascertain the wealth of those territories. The events that followed are common knowledge. In 1521, shortly after the conquest of Tenochtitlán, Cortés ordered Orozco to occupy Huaxyácac, and the town was seized in December of that year. Cortés, convinced of the immense wealth of the region, pressed the Spanish crown to appoint him Marquis of the Valley of Oaxaca. In 1529 the crown duly accorded him the title, and included in his realm the populations of Coyoacán, Cuajimalpa, Tlalpan, Mixcoac, and Tacubaya, south of the Valley of Mexico, the region between today's Cuernavaca and Cuautla, part of the Toluca Valley, the region of Tuxtlas, and, naturally, the Valley of Oaxaca itself and part of the Isthmus of Tehuantepec. Cortés' subjects numbered 23,000.[1]

Ever since, the Oaxaca region has been of fundamental importance to the analysis of the historical development of the indigenous civilization.

Chroniclers and Travelers of the Colonial Era

Among the earliest descriptions of Oaxaca are the *Historia de los indios de la Nueva España,* written in 1533 by a friar, Toribio de Benavente (Motolinía) (c. 1490-1569), who also speaks of Tehuantepec, and the impressions of a Franciscan priest Martín de Valencia of the buildings of Mitla, which he passed through that year.

The *Relaciones Geográficas del Siglo XVI*—a series of official reports published in an early version in 1577, and reprinted with various alterations in 1584—offer reliable information on the territory in question and on the life of nearly all the main indigenous groups in New Spain at the time. The information they contain is based on questionnaires sent to representatives of Phillip II of Spain and to the governors of each province. The *relación,* or report, on Oaxaca is a mine of information on thirty-eight different places in the region, from the Mixtec area to as far as Tehuantepec.

The report on Mitla, compiled by Alonso de Canseco, contains observations on buildings and their roofing, described with such exhaustive precision that, many centuries later, archaeologists would draw on Canseco's account to reconstruct the roof of a section of the Columns Group.

In 1615 Juan de Torquemada (c. 1557-1624) published his *21 Libros Rituales and Monarquía Indiana,* and—though he had never actually seen Mitla—his chronicles refer to what was said by Fray Toribio de Benavente.

Between 1670 and 1674 the Dominican priest Francisco de Burgoa, born in 1600 at Antequera in the Valley of Oaxaca, published two works, *Palestra Historial* and *Geográfica Descripción.* Both of these, despite some discrepancies and a somewhat awkward style, are invaluable aids in the study of the development of Oaxaca from the point of view of ethnographical, archaeological, and historical detail, with special emphasis on the Central Valleys.

Toward the close of the colonial era, the Mexican architect Luis Martín drew out the first ground plan of Mitla, later published by Baron Alexander von Humboldt in his *Ensayo Politico,* illustrated with drawings by Colonel Pedro de Laguna. Humboldt had received this material from the Marquis of Branciforte, the viceroy of New Spain from 1794 to 1797. But despite his descriptions of the buildings of Mitla and comments on their importance, he apparently never set foot in Oaxaca.

Travelers and Expeditions of the Nineteenth and Early Twentieth Centuries

Although by 800 C.E. (Common Era, or since the year 0) Monte Albán was no longer the hub of the economic, political, and religious activities of the Zapotecs, it continued to be seen as a sacred place by the Zapotecs themselves and later by the Mixtecs, who carried out religious ceremonies and made votive offerings there for at least several decades after the Spanish Conquest. Unlike Mitla, which was inhabited, Monte Albán was covered in a thick mantle of earth and vegetation when the Spanish arrived, and therefore failed to draw the attention of the conquistadores, chroniclers, or other travelers during the sixteenth to eighteenth centuries.

At the start of the nineteenth century, Charles IV of Spain instructed Guillermo Dupaix (c. 1750-1818/1820), a captain of Austrian descent, to embark on three expeditions (1805, 1806, and 1807) to track down and give a full account of the archaeological sites in what was still called Nueva España or New Spain. Furthermore, he was to visit Mitla and Monte Albán. The outcome of these expeditions was detailed in *The Antiquities of Mexico,* a volume by Edward Kingsborough, published in London in 1830 and Paris in 1834. It was the first time that anyone had written about Monte Albán, and the text was enhanced with magnificent illustrations by José Luciano Castañeda, showing various buildings and the bas-reliefs of the so-called *danzantes,* together with other archaeological finds.

Toward 1830 the first ground plan of Monte Albán was drawn, and as early as 1863 the buildings were thought to be part of a funerary complex. As for Mitla, in 1830 a German road engineer called Edward Mühlenpfordt made a series of highly detailed drawings of the buildings, used extensively by later authors.

In 1850 a Frenchman, Charles Étienne Brasseur de Bourbourg (1818-1874), visited the region and published a work that mentioned Mitla.

Another Frenchman, Claude-Joseph-Désiré Charnay (1828-1919), took the first photographs of Mitla in 1858-59, and made them public through his volume *Cités et Ruines Américaines: Mitla, Palenque, Izamal, Chichén Itzá, Uxmal,* with an accompanying text by the famous French architect Viollet-Le-Duc.

In 1880 *Les Palais Sacerdotaux de Mitla* was published. One of many works by

Austrian author Teobert Maler, the volume provided exacting descriptions of the city's buildings, which were compared to those of classical antiquity in Europe.

In 1881 the priest José Antonio Gay published his work *Historia de Oaxaca,* in which he discussed the history of the region from its remote origins through to the War of Independence.

William Henry Holmes (1846-1933), a North American and editor at the Field Columbian Museum of Chicago, toured Oaxaca in 1895 and 1897, and published *Archaeological Studies among the Ancient Cities of Mexico,* which included a detailed description of Monte Albán with topographical surveys (so accurate that they seem virtually copied from today's precision maps), complete with drawings of the architectural structures and descriptions of building materials used. These are still visible at the site.

> I climbed the south side by way of a narrow path, controlling my horse with great difficulty. From the main level I then continued up the central pyramid, which is the one crowning this part of the summit, and thus managed to see the magnificent panorama of the mountain and the surrounding valleys. It was three o'clock in the afternoon when I finished the ground plan of the main group, and it was night by the time I reached the main group of the northern complex, after having climbed up, during that time, eighteen of the fifty pyramids included on the map, and having also drawn the various accompanying maps and general views and details. The chain of pyramids runs from north to south toward midway down the large plaza, and constitutes one of the most interesting features of these ruins ... one wonders what the prevailing conditions were during occupation. What the effect must have been of the sight of these pyramids, all of which were crowned with temples ... it is unlikely that civilization ever dreamed up anything similar in so vast and imposing a space as this.[2]

Toward the end of the century Fernando Sologueren and Belmar discovered another eight *danzantes;* the two archaeologists were in fact responsible for giving this name to these bas-reliefs of human figures, and it has remained a standard term ever since. Sologueren, though not originally from Oaxaca, became the constitutional municipal president of the town of Oaxaca in 1912, and donated to the then Museo de Antropología in Mexico City an important collection of archaeological finds from the Oaxaca region, many of which he himself had discovered. Most of the original collection is still in the Museo Nacional de Antropología.

Between 1885 and 1910 the Mexican archaeologist Leopoldo Batres, appointed by Porfirio Díaz to the position of inspector general and curator of the archaeological heritage, completed explorations and reconstructions at Monte Albán and Mitla. In the first site he discovered further representations of *danzantes* and explored part of the North Platform and South Platform, and Building L. In Mitla he cleared away some of the rubble piled up against the Columns Group and began to clear the cross-shaped tomb found in the complex. Concerned about the protection and conservation of the archaeological zone, in 1904 he put up a series of notices in the Hall of Columns forbidding visitors to write on the monuments or damage them.

More or less in the same period Marshall Saville from the American Museum of Natural History in New York carried out some archaeological explorations in the region, and dug out a number of tombs at Xoxocotlán, Monte Albán, and Mitla; he also finished Batres' work on the tomb in the Columns Group. On January 24, 1901, he discovered and shored up the other cross-shaped tomb there.

In 1921 the Dirección de Estudios Arqueológicos y Etnográficos, founded in 1917, cleared away all the modern-day constructions built alongside the Church Group at Mitla, restoring part of the original structure to its former glory.

2. *Danzante* stone bas-relief. From the South Platform at Monte Albán. Monte Albán I. Museo Nacional de Antropología, Mexico City (hereafter referred to as MNA).

3. Cup worked from a single piece of rock crystal. From Tomb 7 at Monte Albán. Monte Albán V. Museo Regional de Oaxaca, Convento de Santo Domingo, Oaxaca (hereafter referred to as MRO).

From 1931 to 1949 Alfonso Caso (1896-1975) directed the longest and most thorough research project ever undertaken at Monte Albán or in the Oaxaca region in general. Caso's stratigraphic surveys provided one of the most comprehensive cultural sequences in Mesoamerica. At the same time, most of the buildings composing the large central plaza at Monte Albán were explored and made safe, and a great many tombs and burials with fine grave goods were discovered, whose pottery facilitated the dating of the monuments.

One of the main purposes of Alfonso Caso's work was to make a detailed study of the pre-Hispanic writing in the codices and inscribed in the stone, in order to establish distinctions between the Mixtec and the Zapotec cultures.

During the earlier excavation campaign of the Proyecto Monte Albán in January 1932, Caso and his collaborators made one of the most remarkable discoveries of Mexican archaeology. This was how Caso himself described the find:

On January 6 we began to explore Tomb 7.... After removing a slab we saw a seashell, thirty-six jade ornaments in two different colors, and three jade earrings; however, there were no human remains associated with these objects.... When we came across the shell and the jade ornaments, we realized that the tomb below must be very well furnished. At four in the afternoon on January 9 we managed to lift one of the slabs that served as a sloping lid for the second funerary chamber. Lowering an electric light through the opening, we were thus afforded a view of a human skull, with two vases nearby, one of which immediately drew my attention as it seemed to be [made] of an unusually smooth, black terra cotta. It was actually made of rock crystal and simply appeared dark owing to the earth it contained. Once we had climbed down into the chamber, the first thing we noticed was a large white alabaster vase in the middle of the second funerary chamber. Although caked with earth, once we shone our lights on it, it proved to be translucent. On the threshold between the two chambers of the tomb, massed with a large pile of bones, we saw a gleam of gold (ornaments, rattles, and so forth), and the arms of one of the corpses was adorned with ten bracelets, six in gold and four in silver. Near the tomb's entrance was a gold diadem [crown] together with the feather crest that once decorated it.... Just as I was about to climb back out of the chamber, I spotted a skull decorated with mosaic in turquoise, lying near the entrance to the first chamber. When we shone our lights on the chamber floor, it sparkled with pearls, gold ornaments and countless *tesserae* [small pieces of glass, marble, or tile] of turquoise, once part of an elaborate mosaic.... As we left the tomb we were absolutely con-

4. Pendants wrought in gold with lamination and filigree technique. From Tomb 7 at Monte Albán. Monte Albán V. MRO.

vinced of the inestimable material, artistic and scientific wealth we had discovered; it occurred to me that nowhere had I read of a discovery—in America—of a find of this magnitude.[3]

Indeed, Caso's discovery of the nine Mixtec individuals buried together with an opulent votive hoard inside a Zapotec tomb brought him worldwide fame, but discussions ensued on the characteristics of the material found, in the course of which the archaeologist was even charged with having deliberately planted the objects for the purpose of achieving recognition.

Caso's research, which involved the assistance of an eminent team of collaborators including Ignacio Bernal and Jorge Acosta, after lengthy and painstaking work facilitated the identification and definition of the most important features of Zapotec and Mixtec culture, such as their pottery, architecture, religion, calendar, and funeral rites. Vital progress was made in deciphering the Mixtec codices; two of Caso's writings refer specifically to these, *El Mapa de Teozacoalco* (1949) and *Reyes y Reinos de la Mixteca,* published in 1977, seven years after the author's death.

To make comparison with other sites possible, Caso carried out an excavation campaign at Mitla and at other sites in the Mixteca Alta, namely Tilantongo, Monte Negro, Yucuñudahui, Yucuita, and Las Pilitas. Besides Bernal and Acosta, Caso's colleagues included Rubín de la Borbolla, Eulalia Guzmán, Martín Bazán, Jorge Valenzuela, Javier Romero, Laurette Sejourné, and Augustín Villagra.

Contemporary Archaeology

In the two ensuing decades from 1950 to 1970 research campaigns fanned out to include sites such as Zaachila, excavated by Roberto Gallegos in 1962, and Lambityeco, excavated by Mexico City College.

After participating in the project organized by Alfonso Caso in 1958, the archaeologist Jorge Acosta directed maintenance and reinforcement works on the structures already brought to light, and took back to Monte Albán a set of fourteen engraved stones which had been housed at the Museo Nacional de Antropología in Mexico City.

Ignacio Bernal, who had previously taken part in the Proyecto Monte Albán, undertook new excavations in Yagul from 1954 to 1962 with Lorenzo Gamio. In 1948 he had been at Coixtlahuaca, and in 1952 at Tamazulapan (Mixteca Alta) as head of the Departamento de Antropología of Mexico City College; soon after, he began ex-

5. Gold fan handle decorated with serpent head. From Tomb 7 at Monte Albán. Monte Albán v. MRO.

cavating at Cuilapan. From 1966 to 1972 he explored Dainzú, where he found a series of fascinating stones engraved with figures playing a ball game.

From this moment on, archaeological work in Oaxaca switched from the exploration of sites and monumental complexes to more theoretical issues, not always related to the main structures of the sites. In 1965 Kent Flannery embarked on the Proyecto de Ecología Humana Prehistórica del Valle de Oaxaca, focusing on the application of theoretical models for explaining the evolution of the various cultural systems. During this project excavations were carried out at San José Mogote, Tierras Largas, Huijazóo, and Fárica San José in the Etla Valley, all important places because they yielded new information on sites predating the foundation of Monte Albán. In 1969 Flannery and his colleagues explored the cavern of Guilá Naquitz near Mitla, where they discovered traces of hunter-gatherers datable to approximately 8000 B.C.E. (Before the Common Era, or before the year 0).

In 1971 Richard Blanton and his colleagues carried out an ambitious scheme involving the study of settlement models in the Valley of Oaxaca, attempting to reconstruct their historical and cultural evolution through the analysis of surface archaeological material; this particular branch of research is still being continued by Kowalewski and Finsten.

In 1972-73 Marcus Winter undertook excavations in an area inhabited in pre-Hispanic times, just north of Monte Albán. Here he studied several domestic units containing burials of individuals with trephined, or surgically cut, skulls. This and later research made it possible in 1974 to establish certain typological characteristics regarding the dwelling units in one sector of Monte Albán.

In the wake of the Caso and Bernal era, Ronald Spores provided additional information in the 1960s on the Nochixtlán Valley in the Mixtec region. In the 1970s Margarita Gaxiola and Marcus Winter undertook new fieldwork at Huamelulpan; in the last few years Winter has carried out valuable new excavations at the site of Cerro de las Minas, near Huajuapan de León.

Further excavation work and restoration in other sectors of the Oaxaca region include investigations by Charles Spencer in the Cañada area from 1977 to 1980; in the Mixteca de la Costa area, the work of De Cicco and Donald Brockington in 1956, and later work by Brockington and associates from 1966 to 1974; at Guiengola on the Isthmus of Tehuantepec work was carried out by David Peterson around 1979; and, finally, during the same period, Enrique Méndez undertook excavations in the Huave area.

During an excavation campaign in 1984 in the Huijazóo area in the Etla Valley Méndez investigated Mound G of Platform 1, where he had come across the first traces of walls forming the access area of a tomb. Continuing his investigations above the north wall he found a *tablero* (a vertical rectangular slab) adorning the entrance; its center is carved with a mask depicting the head of a jaguar-serpent with a bird emerging from its jaws. The entire mask is shielded by clocks of stone perfectly cut to form a kind of box, to avoid damage from falling debris. That year various problems impeded any further exploration and everything was carefully covered back up.[4]

The following year in November 1985, after having completely cleared away the access area, the slab blocking the tomb's entrance was removed. This chamber was later called Tomb 5. The details of this moment were recounted by Méndez:

> I entered the enclosure from the left side (west), covering my mouth and nose with a mask to protect myself from possible intoxication; lighting the way with a torch I noted that at the entrance, near the huge slab of stone, lay the remains of some bones and a pair of *acompañantes,* the urns that accompanied the god, similar to those found in various Zapotec burials. After shining the torch fur-

ther inside I noticed that most of the pottery, deposited as a ritual offering, was broken. Cautiously picking my way forward so as not to disturb anything in my path, I studied the marvelous paintings decorating the interior. In the chamber it was noticeably difficult to breathe, and not without reason: I was the first human to enter the chamber since it had been sealed shut. 1,100 years had passed before this discovery of the finest expression of Zapotec art, the pride of the inhabitants of Oaxaca, of the Mexicans, and of the world of art.[5]

Tomb 5 at Huijazóo is indeed the most important example of funerary architecture in the entire region of Oaxaca (see also Appendix), as it offers an outstanding fusion of diverse elements. In the two antechambers and mortuary chamber, the walls are painted with figures representing deities, priests, high-ranking figures, ball players, warriors, calendrical inscriptions, and so forth. The doorjambs are carved with images of the founding couples of the ruling dynasty, together with other key figures and members of the priesthood, flanked by hieroglyphic inscriptions. Another significant feature is the use of the *tableros a doble scapulario* at the entrance to the main chamber, supporting the masks of stone and stucco with representations of deities in the form of jaguars, serpents, and birds. Finally, at the back of the main chamber there is a genealogical stela of astonishing manufacture engraved with a high-ranking figure seated on a throne and wearing a large headdress typical of Cocijo, the rain god. The tomb complex is a space of extraordinary beauty, reproducing the characteristic layout of the rooms of a house built round a central courtyard; in this way, the home of the dead was akin to that of the living.

After this discovery, the Dirección de Restauración of the Instituto Nacional de Antropolígía e Historia (INAH) intervened to ensure the proper conservation of Tomb 5; given its characteristics, however, it was not possible to leave it open to the public. Now this monument is under the protection of the INAH, and the objects found on the site are on display at the Museo Comunitario de Santiago Suchilquitongo.

Ever since its foundation in 1972, the Centro Regional de Oaxaca of the INAH has engaged a group of researchers working full time who have achieved excellent results in various fields of the anthropological and historical disciplines. Despite this, as with other sites in the region, the archaeological outlook of this center has altered with the changing trends. Ignacio Bernal sums up these trends very clearly:

> Until a few years ago investigations focused on the larger monuments... Now instead they concentrate more on the everyday aspects of the people, discarding the other aspects as "elitist." This is absurd because we need to know as much about palaces as about shacks. In my opinion the archaeologists of the past might be criticized for concentrating on the palatial structures, but today many are only interested in the shacks, precluding the knowledge of some of the most significant remains of the ancient world. If we are not prepared to look at all the aspects of a society of the past, we are unlikely to understand it. Hence the importance of studying all the surviving testaments and trying to investigate the less evident aspects.[6]

In addition to the research undertaken in various parts of the region, the archaeological work of the Centro Regional de Oaxaca has also included the retrieval and safeguarding of important material and information which sometimes remain the only testament of a given site or a particular chronological period. In the past, what interested the researchers when they came to the region was simply to complete their own project, leaving the excavation areas in complete abandon after they were through. The archaeologists of the Centro Regional have made it their task to ensure the surveillance, conservation, delineation, and maintenance of the region's archaeological zones: this type of intervention is less spectacular and often passes unnoticed, but is equally important for archaeology because it enables the gathering of data and material essential for furthering our knowledge of ancient Mexico.

Excavations are currently under way at Huamelulpan and Cerro de las Minas, in the Mixtec area, and likewise at Dainzú, Lambityeco, Mitla, and Monte Albán in the Central Valleys. On Monte Albán, in addition to having excavated and shored up the walls along the south, east, and north of the North Platform, the northeast corner yielded the remains of a building dating from the period known as Monte Albán III, the residence of a priest or other important figure; these structures will provide new information on the social and political organization of the inhabitants of Monte Albán.

6. Remains of a building during excavation. Northeast corner of the North Platform at Monte Albán.

Chapter Two
The Zapotecs

Chapter Two
The Zapotecs

The Environment

The Central Valleys of the Oaxaca region formed the habitat of the so-called Cloud Peoples, known as *Ben Zaa* in the Zapotec tongue. These ancient peoples are termed *Tzapotecatl* in Náhuatl, the *lingua franca* of the Aztecs, but this word was probably never actually used by the Zapotecs themselves.

The Central Valleys are enclosed by high and spectacular mountains on all sides, and enjoy a warm and pleasant climate. In the past there were many average-sized streams, such as the Río Salado, all flowing into the main river, the Atoyac, which conveyed the life-giving resource throughout the land.

Three valleys create an extensive cleft shaped like an upturned Y, 59 miles (95 kilometers) long and 16 miles (25 kilometers) wide, and roughly 4,900 feet (1,500 meters) above sea level. The Etla Valley runs northwest, the Tlacolula Valley southeast, and the Zaachila-Zimatlán south. This vast terrain is bordered in the north by the Sierra Madre Oriental and in the southeast by the mountains of Tlacolula. In earlier times, the soil quality varied—in some areas crop yield depended on the depth of the water table, which was between 10 to 33 feet (3 to 10 meters) below the surface. Where it was not too deep, such as on the plain of the Atoyac River in the Zaachila-Zimatlán Valley, it was possible to dig wells for irrigation. In the Tlacolula Valley the soil was rather arid, whereas the Etla Valley possessed fine alluvial soil which retained water well and was therefore more fertile. In the same valley irrigation was effected with canals, as the Atoyac River ran deep between two high banks.

The valley height ranges from 4,660 feet (1,420 meters) to 5,710 feet (1,740 meters) above sea level. The yearly rainfall also varies from zone to zone, with 19.7 inches (500 millimeters) in some areas and 29.5 inches (750 millimeters) in others. In ancient times the area had a thriving agriculture, with special emphasis on maize, beans, and squash; during the sedentary phase these crops were the staple of the population. Because the sides of the Valley of Oaxaca are not steep, the deforestation activity and conversion of the land for crop-growing did not provoke erosion, as it did in other areas of the Oaxaca region. The average annual temperature of 68 degrees Fahrenheit (20 degrees centigrade), with a fluctuation in the course of the day of 10 degrees Fahrenheit (15 degrees centigrade), made it possible to grow maize

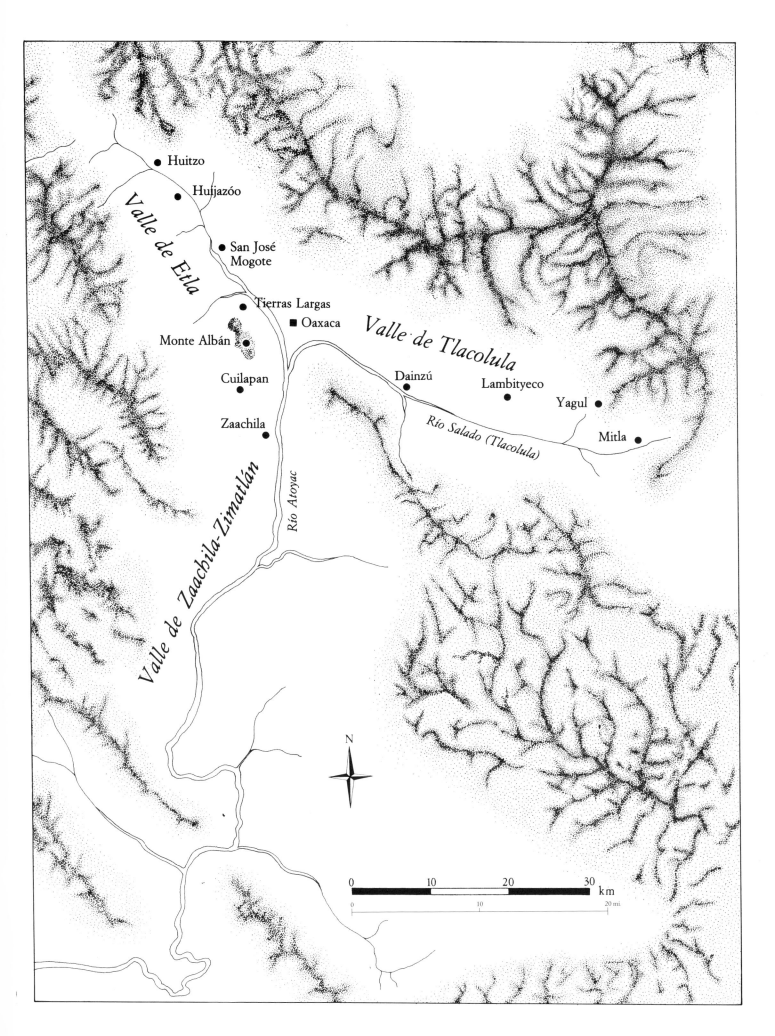

Huitzo

Huijazóo

San José
Mogote

Valle de Etla

Tierras Largas

■ Oaxaca

Valle de Tlacolula

Monte Albán

Cuilapan

Dainzú

Lambityeco

Yagul ●

Río Salado (Tlacolula)

Mitla ●

Zaachila

Valle de Zaachila-Zimatlán

Río Atoyac

N

0	10	20	30

km

0   10   20 mi.

throughout the year. The ecological conditions of the valley were a fundamental impulse to the growth of Zapotec culture.

The Mythical Origins of the Zapotecs

The Zapotec legends, first transcribed in the sixteenth century, claim that the Zapotecs were the original inhabitants of the Valley of Oaxaca, and were born from rocks or from wild animals such as pumas or ocelots. Another legend places their origin further north, from a place called Chicomoztoc, or Seven Caves, which was also the legendary homeland of the Nahua tribes of the Valley of Mexico. This legend shows the possible influence of Aztec culture during the Postclassic Period.

Language

The Zapotec tongue belongs to the family of Otomanguean languages, and began to differentiate itself as a separate language between 4000 and 1500 B.C.E., following the migration and subsequent isolation of various groups. Zapotec is a tonal language, which means that the meaning of a word is often determined by the pitch of the voice. The shifting pitch is combined with closed and open vowels, nasal or staccato sounds, and strong and weak consonants, giving the language a musical sound. The verbs are modified by the addition of suffixes and prefixes to indicate voice (active or passive), tense, and mood. The tenses have various subtle changes in meaning to indicate actions in the past, present, or future.

Zapotec was really a collection of different languages, though it may be that the Zapotecs were originally monolingual. Today, some scholars have specified six languages: Valley Zapotec, Tehuano or Isthmus Zapotec, Serrano Zapotec (spoken on the sierra), Nexitzo or Rincón Zapotec (spoken in the Villa Alta district), Villalteco (from Yalálag), and Miahuatlán Zapotec.

Chronology

On the basis of archaeological studies, particularly those made on pottery, a series of settlement or cultural development phases have been identified: *Monte Albán I,* with three sub-phases A, B, and C, spanning 500-100 B.C.E.; *Monte Albán II,* with two sub-phases A and B, spanning 100 B.C.E. to 250 C.E.; *Monte Albán III,* with two sub-phases IIIA (250-650 C.E.) and IIIB (650-800 C.E.); *Monte Albán IV,* spanning 800-1325 C.E.; and *Monte Albán V,* spanning 1325-1521 C.E.. *Monte Albán II* to IIIA is considered a transitional phase. Earlier chronological phases have been established for the period prior to *Monte Albán I,* and these are *Espiridión* (1900-1500 B.C.E.) *Tierras Largas* (1500-1200 B.C.E.), *San José* (1200-800 B.C.E.), *Guadalupe* (800-700 B.C.E.), and *Rosario* (700-500 B.C.E.). Calculations of the earliest occupations are facilitated by the analysis of pottery types and their correlation to those of other regions; by settlement models and techniques of subsistence; by excavation work in the settlements; and by the delineation of spaces and their uses.

As elsewhere in Mesoamerica, in the Oaxaca region the earliest cultural period is termed Lithic or Preceramic; this was followed by the Formative or Preclassic, Classic, and Postclassic periods. Each of these periods was later split up into sub-phases according to the region in which they were applied. Some authors consider these periods as chronological stages, others as entities of different levels of development in

Opposite page:

7. The three Central Valleys of Oaxaca with their archaeological sites.

29

B.C.E.) that anything definably Zapotec emerged. Others take a different view, however, and argue that Zapotec cultural traits can be traced back to as early as 1400 B.C.E.

The Lithic or Preceramic Period

The Lithic or Preceramic Period was a long one, stretching from 7000 to 1500 B.C.E. There is talk of a climate change around the year 7000 B.C.E., causing a lack of rain, which provoked a transformation of the vegetation, creating conditions similar to those existing today.[4] The extinction of the Pleistocene fauna and the hotter climate meant that the groups of hunter-gatherers turned to hunting smaller animals, fishing, and gathering new types of plants; they also made the first steps in domesticating some wild plants such as squash and primitive maize.

The Formative Period: The Early Villages

The first settlements in the Valley of Oaxaca that reflect what is today termed Zapotec culture date from 1400 B.C.E. and have been found in the river areas. Sites include Tierras Largas, San José Mogote, and Hacienda Blanca.

The Formative Period includes the phases known as Tierras Largas, San José, Guadalupe, Rosario, and Monte Albán I and II. In the Formative Period the indigenous groups became sedentary thanks to the domestication of various plants, which soon led to farming and the birth of villages.

The interval of Village Culture in the Oaxaca regions extends from approximately 1400 B.C.E. to 500 B.C.E., but villages continued to exist in the following centuries, as they do today. The cultural features of the valley groups began to emerge in this period, becoming increasingly varied and complex.

Extensive studies have been made into the origin of the populations of the Valley of Oaxaca. Some authors maintain the theory of slow development of nomadic hunter-gatherers, who became sedentary due to the domestication of plants. According to other researchers, groups already practicing a primitive form of farming migrated to this area and settled there. But the scarcity of definite information makes it impossible to make any conclusive assertions either way. The two processes do not exclude each other and may even have taken place at the same time. Exhaustive research has been carried out in other parts of the world into the origins of agriculture, the links between farming and subsistence, the development of techniques of food preparation and conservation, and irrigation systems; the evidence shows that there is a transition from subsistence economy based on hunting and gathering to a predominantly farming economy.

Tierras Largas, San José Mogote, and Dainzú

The most studied Village Cultures of the Formative Period are Tierras Largas and San José Mogote, situated north of today's town of Oaxaca. The sites chosen by the settlers are mainly concentrated around the rivers where the water table is nearest the surface. Hence most villages are gathered in the Etla Valley and the central part of the Valley of Oaxaca, near Zaachila; by contrast, there are few in the Tlacolula Valley where the water table is much deeper.

Water clearly played a vital role, as all the sites dating to this period are near places where irrigation was feasible. Irrigation involved digging the maize fields with

9. Terra cotta *florero*-type jar with a stylized effigy of the water god Cocijo. Region of Oaxaca. Monte Albán I. MNA.

10. Sketch of a Village Culture dwelling unit from the Formative Period, with maize field, burial, food storage pit, and sunken oven (from Winter, 1989).

wide, shallow wells that quickly filled with water, which was scooped up in large vessels and poured straight onto the plants or into small channels. Cultivation techniques included the practice of a fallowing system.

The crops thus produced were enough to ensure the livelihood of nucleated sedentary villages composed of roughly eight to ten households, as established from studies made at Tierras Largas for the period from 1300 B.C.E. to 900 B.C.E. Also at Tierras Largas calculations made on the basis of the capacity of dwellings and the quantity of artifacts found suggest that a hut could house between two and four people. The houses were 20 to 23 feet (6 to 7 meters) long and 13 to 16 feet (4 to 5 meters) wide.[5]

Funeral rites tend to be of vital use in determining the various aspects of the economic, social, and political organization of the community. In the Central Valleys during the Formative Period (1500-250 B.C.E.) burials tend to correspond to a complex society, with rectangular or oval graves dug into the rock or earth, or bell-shaped pits.

The burials are usually in association with the dwellings or are close by. Many burials contained offerings of grave goods composed of miniature vessels, mortars and pestles, and artifacts used in preparing food; generally, however, grave goods are scarce. An association has been noted between certain types of offerings—such as miniature vessels (perhaps imitating vessels used for domestic purposes) and pestles—and female burials, whereas cylindrical vessels are normally found in association with male burials.

All the burials of this period were primary, i.e., the skeletons maintained an anatomical position. In the tombs the prevalent position was supine; in the pits the skeletons were either seated or laid out. In the pit burials, the body was laid on a layer of stones on the floor of the pit. Between the bones and the floor itself there was a layer of sand and domestic debris. Grave goods, if any, were set at either side of the body, near the head. There is no proof that the pits were constructed exclusively for burying the dead, and the fact that the skeletons are generally found above the true level of the pit floor suggests that the pits originally served as ovens or for some oth-

11. Stone mortar and pestle for grinding maize (from Winter, 1989).

33

12. Structures 19 and 28 at San José Mogote.

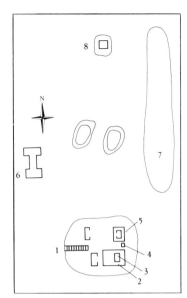

13. Map of San José Mogote.
1) Mound 1.
2) Structure 19.
3) Structure 28.
4) *Danzante* bas-relief.
5) Structure 13.
6) Ball Court.
7) Mound 2.
8) Mound 8.

14. Spout-handled terra cotta jar decorated with a *nadador* or "swimmer" figure. From Monte Albán. Monte Albán I. MNA.

er domestic use. The orientation of the skeletons varies—many were laid east-west, others north-south. Most of the burials from the Formative Period are female.

There is no evidence of ceremonies being performed in the tombs, which would normally indicate social distinctions within the community. When the head of the household died, the house was burned and the site deserted. The most important thing, however, was to remain near one's home; whether one was buried in a pit or a grave was of secondary concern. No burials outside the living precinct have so far been found. The closeness of the burials to the houses continued throughout the Formative Period in the Valley of Oaxaca, and is common to many other parts of pre-Hispanic Mesoamerica.

The complexity of the funerary systems, the differences between votive offerings, together with the definition of the use of space, are all indicative of a society undergoing change.

San José Mogote, a farming village that emerged around 1500 B.C.E., was composed of about fifteen to thirty households. In the San José phase this site boasted several hundred households, and by the Middle Formative Guadalupe phase there were at least 1,500 inhabitants. It clearly became an important center, in which certain high-ranking lineages controlled and redistributed the surplus products from the outlying hamlets, which have been calculated for this period to between twelve and twenty.[6] The village grew from 25 to 100 acres (10 to 40 hectares).

San José Mogote has yielded a great quantity of artifacts including household implements, tools, storage pits, and kilns, complete with figurines, decorated pottery, fragments of black and white mica, mirrors of magnetite, and seashells. Imported items have also been found.

Houses were constructed of wattle-and-daub walls (known locally as *bajareque*) and some had stone foundations. They were separated from one another by courts and patios. Detailed archaeological studies have revealed the whereabouts of the civic buildings, the living complexes, and the areas in which men and women worked. One highly interesting feature was the fact that tools used by women were

34

found to the right as one entered the house, whereas the scrapers, burins (cutting tools), and drills—presumably men's tools—were found on the left.

At San José Mogote a fair number of luxury items were also found, such as magnetite, *Spondylus* shells and pearl-oyster shells, used as personal ornaments; there was also imported pottery. Given their rarity, these objects were clearly not within the means of all the population. This and the other special items present are signs of an emerging differentiation in the society—most of the luxury goods were used by the elite, which began to remove itself from the rest of the population. The products were clearly highly prized possessions, since they came from distant places and hence were rare. The shells came from the Pacific Coast, and other marine products were from the Gulf Coast; material from Chiapas and Guatemala has also been found.

San José Mogote is also the site of the earliest ceremonial zones, including a recessed circular area which had been plastered and painted red, and artificial platforms with stone terrace walls. The artifacts found in these areas are similar to those of the Olmec culture corresponding to Monte Albán I or earlier phases, as are the *danzantes* on stone found at Monte Albán itself, or the bas-reliefs of ball players at Dainzú. Various theories emerged as a result of these parallels. Some suggest that the Oaxaca Valley was invaded by the Olmecs and formed part of an Olmec "empire." Others have suggested that religious pilgrims arrived in Oaxaca to proselytize among the inhabitants. Still others speak of manifestations of Olmec elements—corresponding in time to the Guadalupe phase—as a consequence of exchanges of luxury articles and patterns which enhanced the prestige of the emerging elites in the Valley of Oaxaca and the Olmec area. As Bernal states, while there are definite resemblance between the *danzantes* and the Olmec figures, there are also fundamental differences.[7]

During Monte Albán I there are significant traces of social differentiation, coupled with the centralization of power and growing ceremonial activity. The valley population grew significantly. San José Mogote became particularly important and, during Monte Albán II, reached an extent of over 618 acres (250 hectares). The site also shows signs of the delineation of spaces into ceremonial and non-ceremonial areas, with areas for burial, and others for craftwork.

Dainzú, in the Tlacolula Valley, was also a key site of the Formative Period, and is

15. *Danzante* stone bas-relief. Monument 3, San José Mogote. Rosario Phase (drawing by Mark Orsen, from Blanton, Kowalewski, Feinman, Appel, 1987).

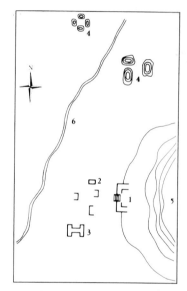

16. Map of Dainzú.
1) Complex A, with bas-reliefs of ball players.
2) Tomb 7, with jaguar lintel.
3) Ball Court.
4) Unexplored mounds.
5) Rocky hill.
6) Seasonal stream.

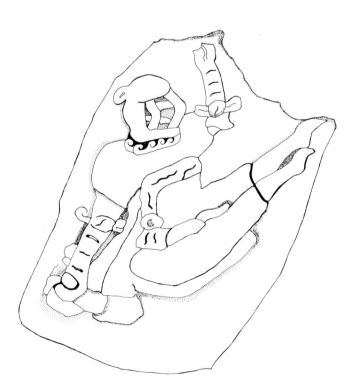

17. Bas-relief with ball player. Dainzú (drawing by Sarah Whitecotton, from Whitecotton, 1984).

thought to have been a seat of power with a highly complex social structure. Excavations carried out by Ignacio Bernal show that Dainzú was occupied approximately from the Rosario phase through the beginning of Monte Albán V. The archaeological site extends to today's village of Macuilxóchitl (which means "five-flowers" in Náhuatl), where it is still possible to see the vestiges of buildings and mounds. Toward the end of the Monte Albán II, Dainzú reached its maximum development and importance. Then the main structures were built, the most important of which includes Complex A, decorated with bas-reliefs of ball players, priests, high-ranking figures, and jaguar-men. They are portrayed in an almost individual fashion and are less severe and military than those in Monte Albán itself. The ball players are caught in dynamic poses, almost like a pre-Hispanic snapshot of the ball game, their protective kneepads drawn in minute detail, along with those for their hands, forearms, stomachs, and heads, which were screened with masks similar to those worn today in football. The ball itself was small enough to fit in the hand. Regrettably, we know nothing of the rules of the game, and this ball court at Dainzú was built in the last phase of the locality's occupation. The depiction of jaguars is a clue to the importance of the site. Further evidence is found on the façade of Tomb 7 at Dainzú, magnificently decorated with a bas-relief jaguar. Although the interior of the tomb was found almost empty, the construction has been dated to Monte Albán II-IIIA.

Another important site is Ayoquesco, south of the Zaachila-Zimatlán Valley.

19. Dog-shaped terra cotta vessel. Region of Oaxaca. Monte Albán I. MNA.

20. Terra cotta tripod vessel engraved with stepped frets, and feet in the form of human heads. From Monte Albán. Monte Albán II. MRO.

21. Terra cotta bowl decorated with multicolored fresco. Region of Oaxaca. Monte Albán II. MRO.

During the final phases of the Formative Period, the Valley of Oaxaca was densely populated, with various regional hubs of power, denominated "independent states." Like the Mixtecs, it appears that the Zapotecs also fostered good relations with the neighboring states through intermarriage and trade, or by creating special alliances (though weak and transitory) while maintaining a strict internal autonomy.

The Classic Period and the Splendor of Monte Albán

Monte Albán was the most important town of Zapotec culture. The origin of its name is unknown, but various hypotheses exist. According to the linguists, the name derives from the word *danibaan,* which in Zapotec means sacred mountain or hill. Some historians maintain that Francisco de Orozco—the Spanish captain under Cortés—gave this name to the town because it resembled certain towns in Italy. Another version has it that a Spaniard by the name of Montalbán was originally the owner of the land, and hence the current name.

Monte Albán is situated at the confluence of the valley branches that form the Valley of Oaxaca, 1,300 feet (400 meters) above the valley bottom and 6,070 feet (1,850 meters) above sea level. Commanding its surroundings, the site is an excellent strategic point and easily defended. Some authors say that during Monte Albán I and II the site also had a defensive wall of roughly 1.6 square miles (2.5 kilometers) along the north, northeast, and west edges of the site, but other authors claim it was part of a reservoir wall for use in the drier months.

The earliest remains at Monte Albán go back to the start of Monte Albán I, but by the following phase of Monte Albán II the settlement already covered 1.5 square miles (4 square kilometers) and harbored the area's most important ceremonial center.

The town was formed by a series of varied constructions spread over a wide area, with separate designated areas for public and private religious ceremonies. Not all the buildings date from the same period. The Grand Plaza and the Danzantes building were begun during Monte Albán I, while most of the buildings still visible today were constructed during Monte Albán III.

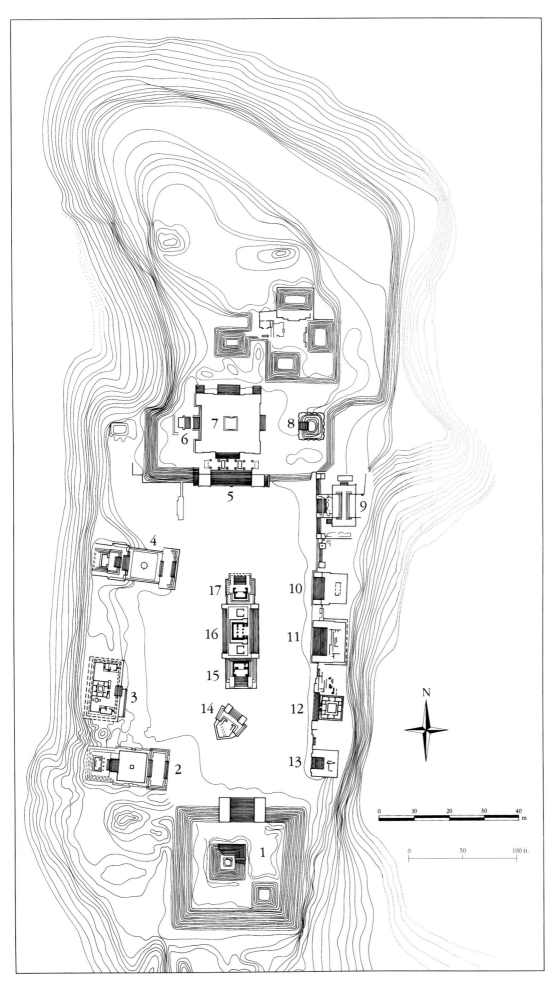

22. Map of the Grand Plaza at Monte Albán (redrawn after Marquina, 1990).

1) South Platform.
2) System M.
3) Danzantes Building, and superimposed Building L.
4) System IV.
5) North Platform.
6) Building B.
7) Sunken patio.
8) Mound A.
9) Ball Court.
10) Building U.
11) Building P.
12) Building S or Palacio.
13) Building Q.
14) Building J or Observatory.
15) Building I.
16) Building H.
17) Building G.

23. The east side of the Grand Plaza at Monte Albán, seen from the north. Mound A is in the foreground.

The Grand Plaza is composed of a rectangular open space surrounded by pyramidal constructions crowned by temples and residences; these were generally created by first building adobe walls, set on stone foundations for added stability. The roofs were flat, supported by a series of beams resting on the walls, on which a matting of canes or palm leaves was laid, followed by a layer of compact earth. This was then covered with a thick mantle of stucco, smoothed off and sloped to let the rainwater run off. Generally the temples comprised two chambers: an antechamber with a spacious entrance and, at the back, another room with a narrower entrance. Certain remains suggest that the walls were originally covered with stucco and painted.

Around the Grand Plaza, which is 660 by 980 feet (200 by 300 meters) along a north-south axis, stands a group of temples, palaces, and other buildings of a political and administrative nature, where the ruling class was lodged. The north and south ends of the plaza are bordered by two large, high platforms with a highly complex architecture, which will be discussed later. The overall effect of the Grand

24. Mound III of the South Platform during excavations. Monte Albán.

Dainzú

1. *General view with the Templo Amarillo in the foreground.*

2. *Tomb 7. Detail of the lintel and doorjambs on the façade, with bas-relief jaguar.*

3. *Complex A, containing the bas-reliefs of the ball players.*

Overleaf:

4. *The Ball Court, only partially excavated.*

Monte Albán

5. *System IV in the Grand Plaza, seen from the southeast.*

Overleaf:

6. *The Grand Plaza, seen from the top of the South Platform. In the center foreground, Building J, the Central Buildings I, H, G, and, in the background, the North Platform.*

7. The west side of the Grand Plaza, seen from the southeast. From left: System M, with the first part in the foreground, and the Danzantes Building.

8. The west side of the Grand Plaza, seen from the top of System M.

9. *The east side of the Grand Plaza, seen from the southwest.* From right: *Building S (or Palacio) and Buildings P and U.*

10. *The Ball Court, on the east side of the Grand Plaza, seen from the south.*

Overleaf:

11. *The Grand Plaza, seen from the northeast.* Foreground, left: *Mound A.* Center: *Buildings G, H, I, and J.* Background: *South Platform.* Background, right: *Building M and part of the Danzantes Building.*

12. *The east side of the Grand Plaza, seen from the north. In the foreground is the Ball Court.*

13. *Probable dwelling on the east side. In the distance is modern Oaxaca.*

14. *The west side of the Grand Plaza, seen from the northeast. In the foreground is the sunken patio of the North Platform, with System IV beyond it.*

15. *Constructions between the west side of the North Platform and Tomb 104.*

Overleaf:

16. *The first part of System M, seen from the northwest. In the background is the South Platform.*

17. 18. 19. *Three views of Building J (or Observatory) set along the central axis of the Grand Plaza.*

Overleaf:

20. *Buildings I, H, and G, along the central axis of the Grand Plaza, seen from the southwest.*

21. *The North Platform, seen from the southwest.*

22. *The Grand Plaza, seen from the north. In the foreground is the sunken patio of the North Platform.*

Overleaf:

23. *System IV, seen from the southeast.*

24. 25. *The Ball Court in the*
Grand Plaza, seen from the
southwest (top) *and from the*
north (bottom).

Opposite:

26. *Stela at the top of the steps*
to the Ball Court.

Mitla

27. *The Hall of Columns. Inside the access hall with the large monolithic columns, which once supported a roof.*
28. *The Hall of Columns, seen from the north.*

Opposite:
29. *The Hall of Columns. Façade of the access hall, seen from the southeast.*

Pages 62-65:
30. *The Hall of Columns. Façade of the access hall, from the south, and part of the North Patio of the Columns Group.*
31. *Inner courtyard of the Hall of Columns.*

32. 33. *Stepped fret decorations on the Hall of Columns.*
34. *The North Building in the large South Patio of the Columns Group. The entrance to Tomb 1 is visible in the base section.*

35. *Inside Tomb 1.*

Opposite:

36. *The Church Group. Southwest corner of the North Patio. Behind it is the Catholic church built by the Spanish in the South Patio, using stone from the ancient Zapotec buildings.*

Overleaf:

37. *The Church Group. The northwest corner of the North Patio.*

Lambityeco

38. Above: *Back view of Mound 195.*

39. 40. Right and opposite: *Details of buildings in Mound 195.*

Yagul

44. *The first slopes of the Yagul hillside, seen from the top of the Fortress, with the valley road leading south.*

Overleaf:

45. *Overview from the east. On the left is the Ball Court; in the center, the Palace of the Six Patios.*

46. 47. Above: *The Palace of the Six Patios, seen from the north.* Right: *The Palace of the Six Patios, seen from the west.*

Opposite:

48. *The Ball Court, seen from the west, is the largest in all of Oaxaca.*

49. 50. The entrance to two
tombs with stepped fret
decorations.

25. *Danzante* stone bas-relief, from System M at Monte Albán. MNA (drawing by Mark Orsen, from Blanton, Kowalewski, Feinman, Appel, 1987).

Plaza is one of breathtaking harmony between the open space and the surrounding constructions, a model of balance and proportion among the individual elements and their broader spatial context, especially considering the buildings and stelae (carved stone slabs or pillars) were only completed at the close of Monte Albán II-IB, after several centuries of concerted effort on the part of the inhabitants. The central buildings break up the vast plaza, achieved artificially, adding to the urban symmetry and vistas against the backdrop of the majestic Valley of Oaxaca. Without exaggerating, it is one of the most beautiful ancient plazas and complexes in the world.

THE DANZANTES BUILDING

Among the buildings bordering the west side of the Grand Plaza stands one of the oldest constructions of all, the Danzantes Building, given this name because of its bas-reliefs of human figures decorating the southeast wall. The figures show naked men in different positions, their genitals exposed or apparently mutilated. There are various interpretations of their meaning. Some say they are invalids or deformed people, others that they are engaged in a ritual dance, and some that they are slaves or prisoners of war. Others suggest that some of the figures represented were *caciques,* or chieftains, of the valley peoples who did not agree with the foundation of Monte Albán as a center of power, and were therefore mutilated and paraded before the public. Today this last version seems the most likely. Together with the *danzantes,* the bas-reliefs include a set of calendrical glyphs that could refer to the year in which the prisoner was captured or mutilated. It is interesting to note that these representations date back to Monte Albán I, and that the stones were later reused for other buildings, taking account of the artwork. The Danzantes Building was surmounted by a larger structure, Building L, corresponding to Monte Albán III.

BUILDING J

The reutilization of some of the masonry with the *danzantes* carvings can be seen in Building J, one of the most interesting, situated along the central axis of the Grand Plaza, on the south side, in front of the South Platform. This is the only construction oriented toward the northeast, and unique owing to its pentagonal floor plan, which could be an architectural interpretation of the year-glyph, which resembles an interlocking A and O. At first it was thought that Building J was a kind of astronomical observatory. Subsequent studies seemed to suggest that the type of relief designs on the walls were there to indicate military victo-

26. Stela 12 with glyphs and numbers. Danzantes Building, Monte Albán (from Willey, 1966).

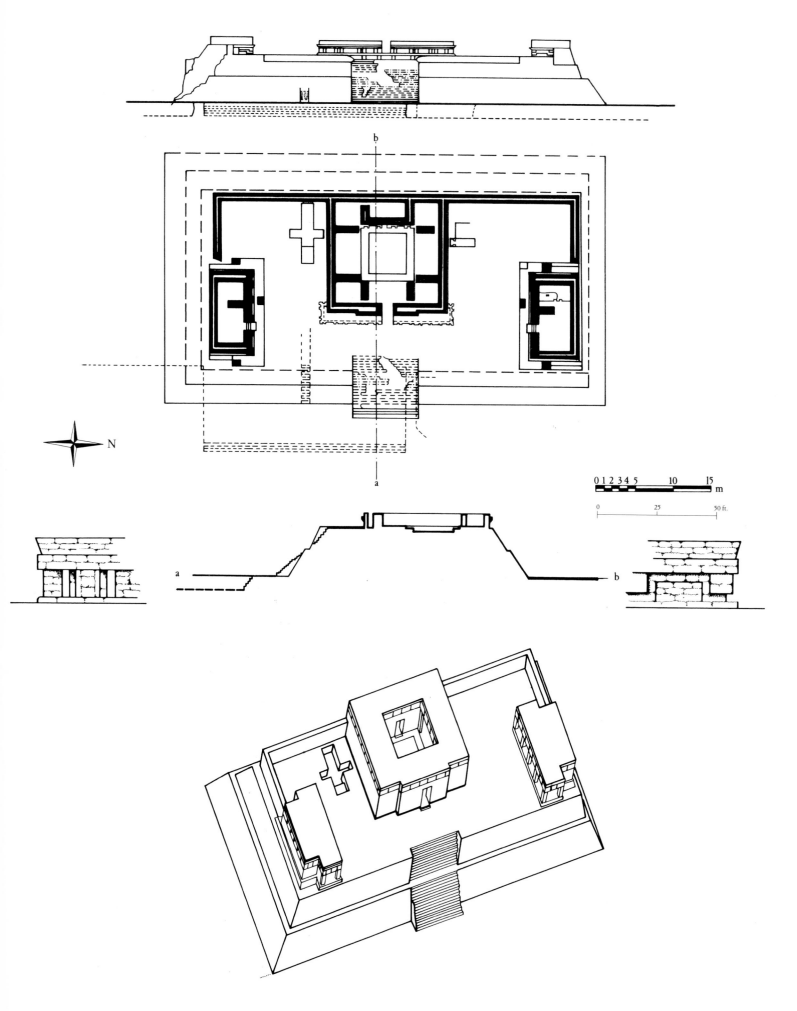

N

82

ries, or the conquest of various villages or chiefdoms, but most people continue to call the building by the misleading name of Observatory. According to Joyce Marcus,[8] most of the stones contain the following elements: (1) a mountain glyph, meaning "the place of"; (2) one or more glyphs representing the name of the place or mountain indicated; (3) an upside-down human head beneath the mountain glyph, symbolizing the governor or people subdued; (4) occasionally a hieroglyphic text which, when complete, includes the year, the month, and the day, together with other glyphs. Marcus has also compared these glyphs against those that appear in the *Codex Mendoza,* and has hence managed to identify the sites of Miahuapan, Cuicatlán, Tototepec, and Ocelotepec, among others. Briefly, the decorations in Building J would therefore be a discourse on political power, addressed not merely to the governing elite of Monte Albán but to the entire

Opposite page:

27. Danzantes Building, and the superimposed Building L, Monte Albán. *From top:* elevation, plan, section, detail of base of central building *(left)* and of the base of the two side buildings *(right),* perspective reconstruction (redrawn after Marquina, 1990).

28. Building J, Monte Albán. *From top:* section, south façade, north façade, plan. *Right and left:* detail of *danzantes* with glyphs, reused in the construction of the building itself (redrawn after Marquina, 1990).

83

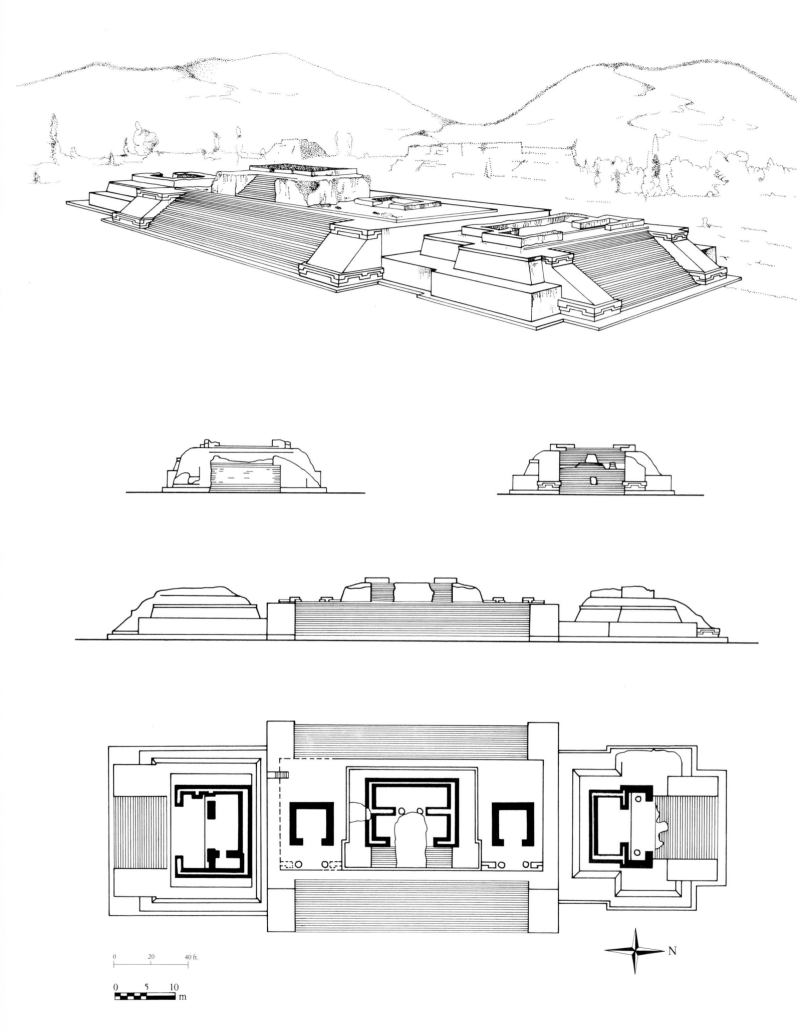

population, which doubtless had access to the Grand Plaza. The date glyphs and the identification of the places engraved on the stonework substantiate this theory.

SYSTEM IV AND SYSTEM M

On the west side of the plaza, to the left and right of the Danzantes Building, are two almost matching buildings: System IV to the north, and System M to the south. Both are composed of an approximately square pyramidal base with a central access stairway lined with broad *alfardas* (sloping ramps on either side of the stairway), and built in stepped blocks with extraordinary examples of *tableros* with *doble escapulario* (i.e., two planes with rectilinear pendants), an architectural peculiarity of the Oaxaca region and with all probability influenced by the architecture of Teotihuacán. At the top stood a one-room temple with stone columns on either side of the entrance. In front of the pyramid base was a rectangular platform, also decorated with *tableros*. The base and the platform are joined by two walls to form a court 100 feet (30 meters) square, with an *adoratorio* or shrine at the center. Both System IV and System M were without doubt dedicated to important deities and witnessed ceremonial gatherings—a limited number of participants in the court, but a larger public in the temple.

Opposite:

29. Central buildings I, H, and G at Monte Albán. *From top:* perspective, south elevation *(left)* and north elevation *(right),* east elevation, plan (redrawn after Marquina, 1990).

30. Place and date glyphs on a slab in Building J at Monte Albán (from Willey, 1966).

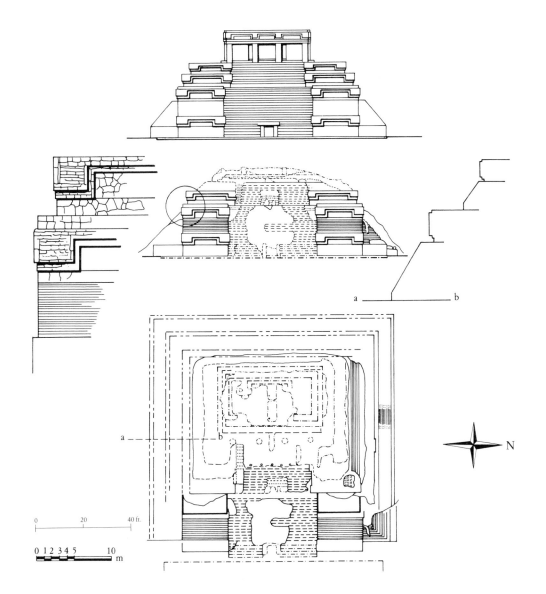

31. Pyramidal body of System M, Monte Albán. *From top:* reconstruction, elevation, detail of *tableros (left),* partial section of base *(right),* plan (redrawn after Marquina, 1990).

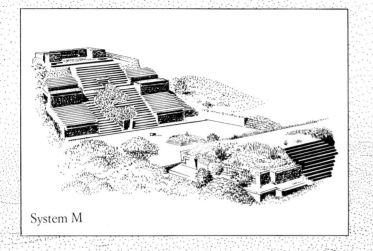

System M

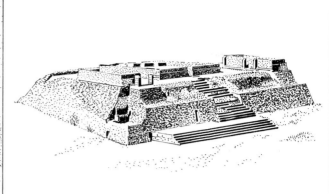

Danzantes Building, and superimposed Building L

South Platform

Building J

System IV

Sunken patio of the North Platform

Ball Court

east-west direction—which chronologically corresponds to the last period of occupation of Monte Albán III, although there are constructions dating from phase I (the period of foundation) to phase IIIB, as shown by the work carried out by Caso and his colleagues.[10]

Facing the Grand Plaza, the North Platform's monumental stairway is flanked by *alfardas* and also decorated with *tableros.* The top of the stairway terminates in a porch with twelve columns, which originally supported a large roof as wide as the stairway. The porch leads down, via a narrower stairway, to a sunken court surrounded by buildings. At the center of the platform stand two temple complexes whose size and position make them the most important of the entire site. At the northeast corner of the platform is a large flat space which is only now being excavated.

In 1990 the Proyecto de Excavación y Mantenimiento de Monte Albán, directed by the author and funded by the Instituto Nacional de Antropología e Historia, established learning more about the function and chronology of the North Platform as one of its primary objectives. In what way did the platform influence, spatially and functionally, the siting and distribution of the residences of the priesthood and other potentates? If this platform was the largest on the site and contains important temple complexes, it must logically contain the remains of the living quarters of the priests who officiated at the ceremonies. Furthermore, we wondered what sort of role was played by the personages who lived in the houses that yielded Tombs 56 and 105 (east), 103 and 104 (north), both of which were built less than 100 feet (30 meters) from the North Platform, though with enormous differences regarding their contents, especially in the tombs.

Excavations begun in 1990 and still under way have brought forth valuable new data. First, a house was found in the upper part of the northeast corner of the platform, near to the main temple complex. The house is composed of four main rooms built around a court with an altar in the middle; this may have been the home of a priest. The east wall was plastered externally, and formed a large court. Rainwater was carefully channeled off through drains into the central court and from here outside the building toward the base of the platform by means of covered conduit. The room on the east side and other buildings alongside are slightly higher than the

35. Detail of the front section of System M, Monte Albán. On the right is the access stairway to the North Platform.

court. The pottery recovered corresponds to Monte Albán II, II-IIIA, and IIIA, and includes a fair amount of material from Teotihuacán, indicating the prestige enjoyed by the dwelling's occupant. Continuing our explorations, we came across the remains of a stairway that may have led to a temple below. Stratigraphic tests showed years of subsequent alterations indicated by the different layers of stucco.

Still on the North Platform, excavations were made on the northeast corner, which is rounded like the southeast corner, with a first section made of rectangular blocks of stone built against the wall. On the north side of this corner is a stairway leading to a wide ledge. On the east side is a rectangular structure, at first thought to be part of the platform itself but later discovered to have a decorative section of *tableros* on the side attached to the platform (west); it was not until Monte Albán II-IB that the three stepped sections were added, uniting it to the North Platform.

Further exploration of the north end of the platform was equally revealing, when the part facing the house of Tomb 104 was excavated to see if there were any links between the two constructions. It became clear that this part of the platform underwent various alterations to the proportions of the stepped sections, but was never actually equipped with a stairway. Therefore, despite the patent importance of his rank as shown by the architecture and decoration of his burial chamber, the person buried in Tomb 104 never had direct access to the temples on top of the platform: he was obliged to go around it and climb the east stairway, passing in front of the house excavated this year, which was very close to the temples. Also during the 1990 excavations, a careful survey of the house with Tomb 56, originally discovered by Alfonso Caso in 1953, revealed two pottery kilns dating from Monte Albán II, and, at the south end, a burial with a woman and two children. Near the woman's skull were several projectile points.

The Postclassic Period: The Militarist Era

The Monte Albán IV phase saw sweeping changes throughout Mesoamerica. At Monte Albán itself, as in the other major pre-Hispanic townships, the transformations attest to serious rifts in society. The people gradually abandoned the large political and administrative hub, and by 900 C.E. it was utterly deserted. It is important to understand what provoked such drastic and irreversible change, and the fact that it happened everywhere at more or less the same time is clearly significant.

Conclusions reached by scholars of the civilizations of Teotihuacán, the Maya, the Zapotecs, etc., vary but are substantially alike: the causes lie in demographic pressure, social unrest, changes in the climate, armed conflict, invasions, and technological imbalances.

John Paddock argues that the crisis in Monte Albán was triggered when the population outgrew its food resources; this was aggravated by undue attention to religious and artistic practices, overlooking the need to find new ways of producing food. According to Richard Blanton, however, Monte Albán was abandoned as a consequence of the fall of Teotihuacán—because the metropolis had never pursued an expansionist policy in the Valley of Oaxaca, Monte Albán had quite simply been abandoned. Blanton does not explain, however, what caused the collapse of Teotihuacán.

In the author's opinion, the causes of the crisis were both material and ideological, with special emphasis on the second. The problems of farming, trade, and taxes were clearly a source of constant pressure on Monte Albán, but the most convincing explanations for its demise lie in the realm of ideology: with the population's dwindling interest in the primary deities, their representatives the priests also fell out of favor and were unable to maintain both a homogeneous political structure and an economic monopoly at the same time.

38. Travertine slab found in Mound X at Monte Albán, called the Lápida de Bazán after its discoverer. It is carved with numerous glyphs and two figures, one Teotihuacán-style, and one typically Zapotec. Monte Albán IIIA. MNA.-

So far, archaeological investigations at Monte Albán have shed little light on phase IV, but elsewhere in the Valley of Oaxaca sites have yielded precise data indicating that when Monte Albán was abandoned other places continued to be inhabited.

During Monte Albán V, the town, now abandoned, was used as a sacred place for offerings to the gods and for burying the dead: proof of this came with the discovery of burials and tombs with funerary offerings of a different style than the ones of phase IV. Thanks to the objects and artifacts found in these burials, we know that the Mixtecs used Zapotec tombs at Monte Albán to bury their forefathers together with rich arrays of grave goods, such as the finely worked and decorated colored Mixtec pottery, engraved bones, and ornaments in gold and silver.

As in other places throughout Mesoamerica, during phase V in the Valley of Oaxaca there was a spread of militarism. The artistic styles are not altogether consistent and it is not possible to distinguish accurately the dominant sites or groups who retained power. We can only distinguish a series of places each with their own style, of a strictly local character.

It has been said that the fall of Monte Albán gave rise to a power vacuum that was hard to fill. The Postclassic Period was characterized by political instability, repeated upheaval, and frequent social and cultural turbulence. The Zapotecs expelled from Monte Albán and those living in the valley towns were constantly struggling among themselves and against outsiders, such as the Mixtecs and Aztecs, who stormed into the Valley of Oaxaca.

In this new situation the Zapotecs tried to establish political cohesion, creating a center of political power at Zaachila, which the Aztecs called Teozapotlán. Mitla meanwhile consolidated itself, and became a major center of religious authority, assuming the role Monte Albán had performed during its heyday.

Mitla: The Great City of the East Valley

Mitla is situated in the Tlacolula Valley, 25 miles (40 kilometers) southwest of today's town of Oaxaca. Mitla is particularly worthy of attention because it was one of the leading Zapotec towns during the Postclassic Period. The buildings on the site are in five main groups, interspersed with the houses of common townsfolk. The layout of the main complexes—the Church Group (or North Group), the Columns Group, the Adobe Group, the Arroyo (stream) Group, and the South Group—is somewhat haphazard, filling the natural spaces available near the river. Unlike at other sites, there is no precise urban plan to the central axis and no established layout model.

The Church Group, the Columns Group, and the Arroyo Group are composed of buildings with the same structure, namely, of long halls with three entrances arranged around a rectangular central patio, which can be either open or closed. Decoration is done with Zapotec *talud-tablero* incorporated with various stepped fret motifs. The Church and Arroyo Groups have three patios.

The Columns Group has only two patios, but the hall on the North Patio, known as the Hall of Columns, is twice the depth of the others, and contains six enormous monolithic columns, which originally sustained a huge wooden beam bearing the smaller beams for the flat roof. Leading off this main hall is a narrow corridor leading to an inner court. Four rectangular rooms look onto the court, all decorated inside and out with *tableros* and stepped frets. According to the descriptions made in the colonial era, these apartments harbored the head priest, who lived in almost total seclusion, out of sight of the common people and communicating with the outside only through his adjutants. In the South Patio of the Columns Group the entrances to two tombs were discovered, built under the halls of the north and east side. They are ossuaries (depositories for bones of the dead) rather than tombs, with a cruciform, or cross-shaped, plan, and walls decorated with *tableros* and stepped frets.

The Adobe Group and the South Group, very much alike, are composed of a square central patio, bordered on the west by a larger pyramidal base, and on the north, east, and south sides by three lower rectangular platforms. These two complexes were the only ones in which mass gatherings took place, open to all the population.

39. Plan of Mitla.
1) Church Group.
2) Columns Group.
3) Adobe Group.
4) Arroya Group.
5) South Group.
6) Stream.
7) Río de Mitla.
A) North Patio of Church Group.
B) Hall of Columns.
C) North Patio of Columns Group.
D) South Patio of Columns Group.

Opposite page:

40. *Top right:* Plan of Palace of Columns, Mitla.
1) Hall of Columns.
2) Corridor.
3) Inner court.
4) Living quarters.

41. *Top left:* Perspective section of the Hall of Columns at Mitla, and a detail of the stepped fret decorations on the building's *tableros* (redrawn after William Holmer, Marquina, 1990).

42. *Middle right:* Plan of the South Patio of the Columns Group at Mitla (from Kubler, 1984).
1) Tomb 1.
2) Tomb 2.

43. *Middle left and bottom:* South Patio of the Columns Group at Mitla. Sectional perspective of the north hall showing Tomb 1 beneath, with detail of stepped fret decorations (redrawn after William Holmes, Marquina, 1990).

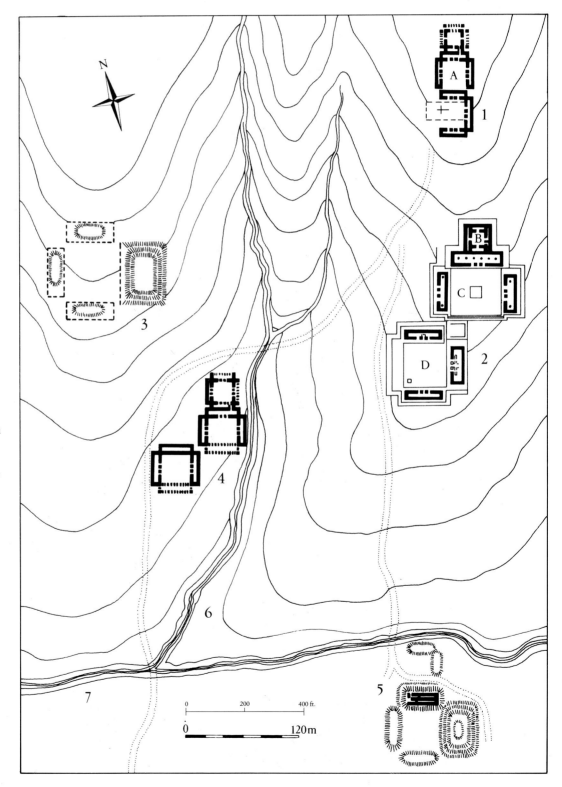

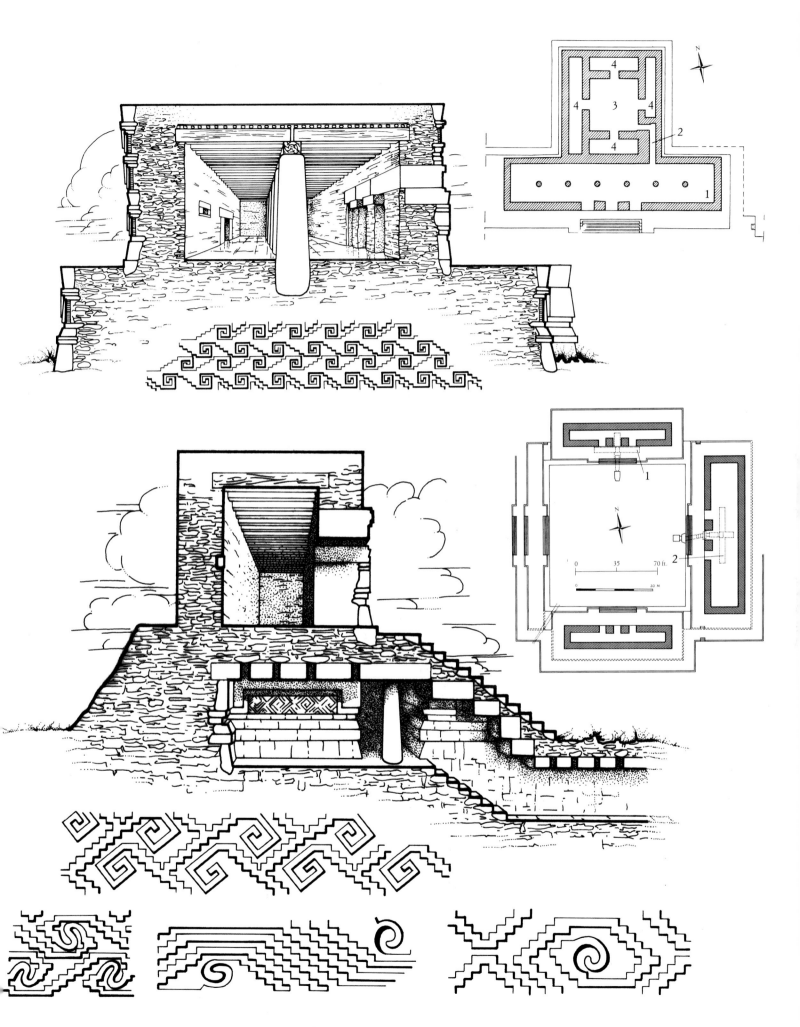

Unlike many other sites in Oaxaca and throughout Mesoamerica, Mitla has yielded no signs of a ball court, though the game may have been played in the open.

Much of what we know of Mitla comes from the *Relaciones Geográficas del Siglo XVI* recorded by the Spanish. The text describes Mitla as a large ceremonial center with a primordial cult for ancestors; as the last refuge for the nobility and priesthood; and as the palace or residence of the high priest and his adjutants. On the basis of what we know and what remains of Mitla, we may infer that during this period the people continued to put much faith in religious matters, and even the military leaders were obliged to submit to the consent of the priesthood. And yet religion had become an intimate family concern, losing its ability to draw gatherings; for this reason there was no further justification for the erection of large temples during the Postclassic Period.

Lambityeco

Lambityeco is another important Zapotec center, contemporary with Monte Albán. It continued to be inhabited long after the latter was abandoned. Lambityeco is situated in the Tlacolula Valley and offers a magnificent example of a village from phase IIIB-IV. As in Mitla, the priority of civic buildings over religious structures is evident.

The occupation of the site probably dates to the Rosario phase (700-500 B.C.E.), shortly before the foundation of Monte Albán, and lasted through to 800 C.E. It was part of a larger settlement called Yeguih. The inhabitants of Lambityeco made their living from the production and export of salt, obtained by boiling the salt-bearing ground water in large terra cotta vessels called *apaxtles*. The village's stucco sculptures are of astonishing beauty, some with highly realistic detailing.

Two buildings belonging to the local elite have been partially explored and restored. The first, called, according to some authors,[11] the House of Coqui, or the Lord's House, is on Mound 195 and has a highly distinctive set of stucco portraits of the building's owners, as if to endorse the emphasis on worldly rather than religious matters. The *tableros* on either side of an altar in the courtyard are decorated with two stucco bas-reliefs. The one on the left shows a certain 4 Face holding a human femur in his hand, alongside a female figure, 10 Monkey; on the right *tablero* is 3 Turquoise and her male companion 8 Owl. Opposite the altar stands Tomb 6 in which the remains of several generations of governors were buried with their consorts. The façade of the tomb is adorned with the most well-known Zapotec *tablero* with a cornice in two planes with rectilinear pendants, decorated with two stucco heads representing the lord 1 Earthquake and his lady 10 Reed (see color plate 43). The tomb yielded the remains of six individuals and 186 associated objects.

44. *Tablero* decorated with stucco figures representing Lady 3 Turquoise and Lord 8 Owl. Mound 195, Lambityeco.

The second building, 49 feet (15 meters) from the previous one, on Mound 190, was probably the abode of the *bigaña* or chief priest. It contains a central altar between two courtyards and is decorated with *tableros* of large masks of sculpted stone and stucco representing Cocijo, the god of rain and thunder, who features frequently in Zapotec iconography. The masks are all alike, and measure 3 feet (1 meter) across. The few surviving examples show details of the rain god: the mask covering most of his face and encircling his eyes like spectacles, the large patch over his nose, and the bulky plumed headdress with two jutting sections adorned at the tips with greenstone insets.

Lambityeco was abandoned during a moment of political upheaval following the demise of the Zapotec hegemony triggered by battles and internal struggles—events which drove the inhabitants to look for more strategic sites that could be more effectively defended.

Yagul

Founded in Monte Albán I, Yagul did not become important until phase V, the period in which the number of inhabitants and buildings increased. The first traces of occupation on the site are found on a rocky outcropping known as Caballito Blanco, close to Lambityeco. During Monte Albán II the promontory saw the construction of a pointed temple very similar to Building J at Monte Albán (the only buildings

45. Stone and stucco mask representing the god Cocijo. Mound 190, Lambityeco.

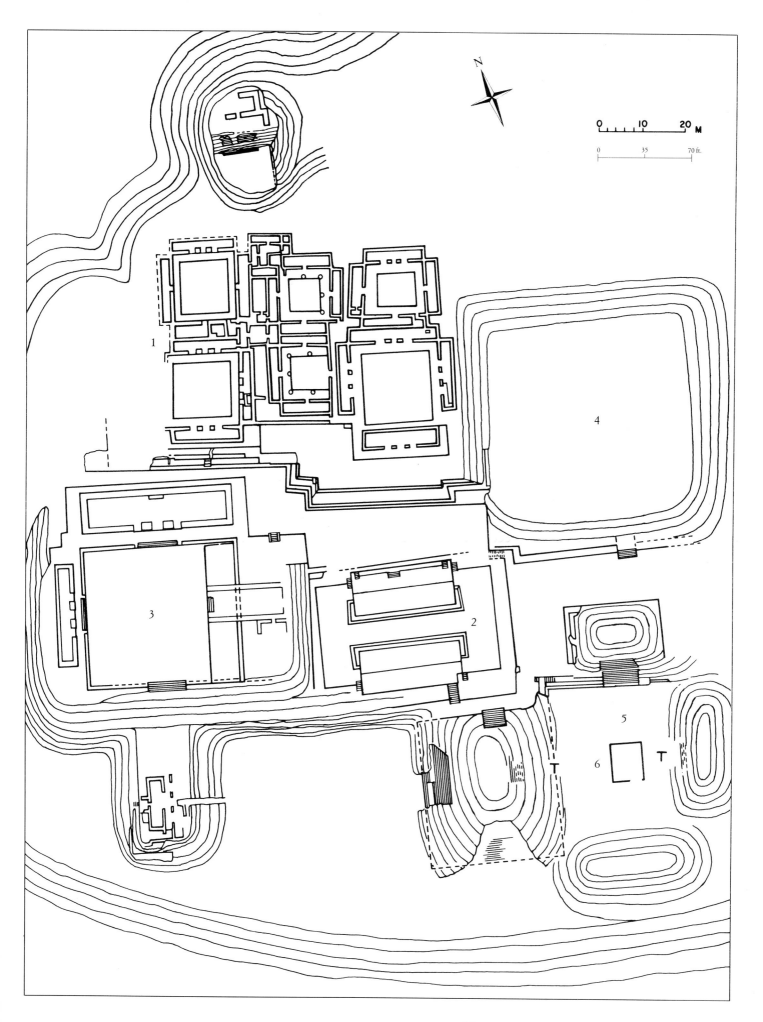

with this kind of base). During phase V the settlement was shifted a several hundred feet further north, to a ledge of volcanic tufa. Here the first group of houses were built, together with bases and the largest stadium for ball games in the Oaxaca region. On a rise at the northern end of this plateau the inhabitants built a small defensive wall of dry stone to shield them from attacks in that direction. The system of construction used for the wall and fortress is similar to that used in Mitla; the same applies for the dimensions and pattern of the rooms around the central courtyards, some covered, others open.

In Yagul the union of the architecture with the environment is perfect: the constructions descend in broad terraces giving an impression of solidity and magnificence. The buildings open for view today are from Monte Albán V, and were built over others from the previous phases.[12]

According to some authors, during the transitional period from Monte Albán IV to V, Lambityeco was abandoned due to political turbulence and strife in the region; the inhabitants apparently moved to Yagul in search of greater security. In both sites the population was of Zapotec origin, though at Yagul there are traces of Mixtec material, resulting from intermarriage or military alliances.[13]

Huijazóo

A small site toward the northeast rim of the Etla Valley in the great Central Valley of Oaxaca, Huijazóo is attracting increasing attention. The site, also known as Cerro de la Campana, is situated on the summit of a small hill sculpted with human-made terracing. The village faces south and covers 1.2 square miles (3 square kilometers). Although there are traces of occupation beginning with Monte Albán I, the site's peak of splendor was achieved in phase IIIB-IV. Two groups comprising about forty buildings and bases linked by stuccoed access routes proceed up the steep hillside. The main nucleus, perched on the highest peak, Cerro de la Campana, is composed of a ball court and three distinct complexes, with courtyards and mounds not yet fully explored.

Given the situation, Huijazóo was probably a compulsory watering place for traders up and down the long route between Monte Albán and the towns of the Cañada and Mixteca regions. According to the studies of the Dominican friar Francisco de Burgoa,[14] toward the end of phase IIIB-IV the site became a bastion against the raids of the Mixtecs, who aimed to dominate the valley. The discovery of a Zapotec tomb under Mound G by the archaeologist Enrique Méndez in 1985 prompted new questions on the abandonment of Monte Albán and the role of secondary sites such as Huijazóo.[15] The vast resources required in the construction of Tomb 5--with its splendid murals, bas-reliefs, and *tableros* decorated with stucco masks—were supplied by a family rich enough to afford a more sumptu-

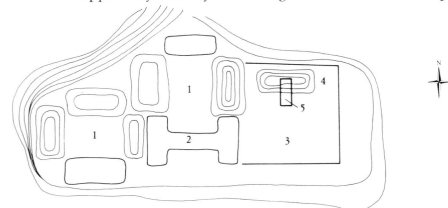

Opposite page:

46. Map of Yagul (from Paddock, 1970).
1) Palace of the Six Patios.
2) Ball Court.
3) Patio One.
4) Patio Three.
5) Patio Four.
6) Triple tomb.

47. Partial plan of main center of Huijazóo.
1) Patio with partially explored mounds.
2) Ball Court.
3) Platform 1.
4) Mound G.
5) Tomb 5.

a cross-shaped plan, and so forth. Sometimes there was more than one niche. Facades came in different forms—a simple vertical wall, a wall decorated with a full, plain, or stepped cornice set over the entrance lintel, or a *tablero* wall, and so on. Each of these features was typical of a distinct phase of occupation, though some features continued to be in use and were occasionally combined with new models.

All the tombs from Monte Albán I[17] have roofs of large horizontal slabs, and are without entrances, niches, or facades, in the style of the *cajón.* They are oriented in a north-south or east-west direction. This type of tomb, more or less with the same architectural elements, remained the standard until phase IIIB, the only difference being the kind of offering deposited.

The most common type of tomb during Monte Albán II[18] was still the flat-roofed, nicheless *cajón,* but now it had an entrance. There were, however, significant changes to the funeral architecture, as there were in other aspects of Zapotec artistic expression. A new introduction was the sloping roof, formed with large slabs giving a typical pointed roof resting on the walls of the tomb; this kind of roof was sometimes used in combination with the flat type. The antechamber also makes its appearance. Characteristics of this period include tombs with niches but no doorjambs, with no distinction between the antechamber and chamber proper, giving the impression of a single space. The facades during this period were vertical. Earthen floors gave way to stucco floors. Access stairways appeared, usually in connection with antechamber tombs. There was also a predominance of tombs with three niches.

During Monte Albán III[19] a significant change was the introduction of murals on the interior walls of the tombs. These are usually complex groups of symbolic figures featuring deities or priests with their relative glyphs. The oldest funerary mural found so far is in Tomb 72 in Monte Albán (phase II-IIIA), with its series of red glyphs. In some cases processions of men or women are portrayed, singing during some religious ceremony, as seen in Tomb 5 at Huijazóo (phase IIIB). The murals are highly colored, with a predominance of red hues, ochers, white, green, turquoise, light blue, and black.

The murals from phase IIIA (such as those in Tomb 105 at Monte Albán) bear a certain resemblance to those of Teotihuacán, though the style is clearly Zapotec. The paintings from phase IIIB, less similar to those of Teotihuacán, are smaller and less refined.

In this era earlier murals were frequently painted over with new pictures, executed by masters in the art of mural painting. One example is Tomb 105 at Monte Albán, which has superimposed layers of painting. Not all the tombs were repainted, however. In Tomb 104 at Monte Albán (phase IIIA-IIIB) the original paintings were not disturbed; the daubs and splashes of pigment suggest that they were completed rather hurriedly, however.

During Monte Albán IIIB, new tomb styles emerge, with mixed flat and sloping

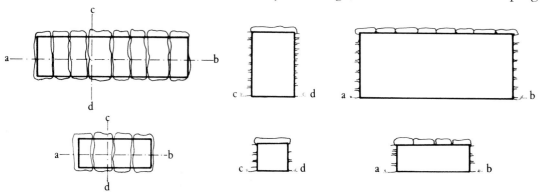

56. Plan and sections of Tombs 43 *(top)* and 33 *(bottom)* at Monte Albán. Phase I (redrawn after Marquina, 1990).

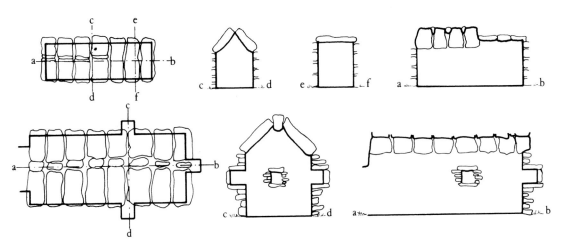

57. Plan and sections of Tombs 135 *(top)* and 77 *(bottom)* at Monte Albán. Phase II (redrawn after Marquina, 1990.

slabs covering a rectangular floor plan with entrance and simple corners; a new type then appears with corners with pyramidal front and back, characteristic of this particular phase. Antechambers were less common, but earthen floors became the norm, and the composite *tablero* façade was first introduced. The number of niches varied considerably, reaching up to five for this period. The tombs themselves are generally aligned east-west and only a few north-south, though most continued to

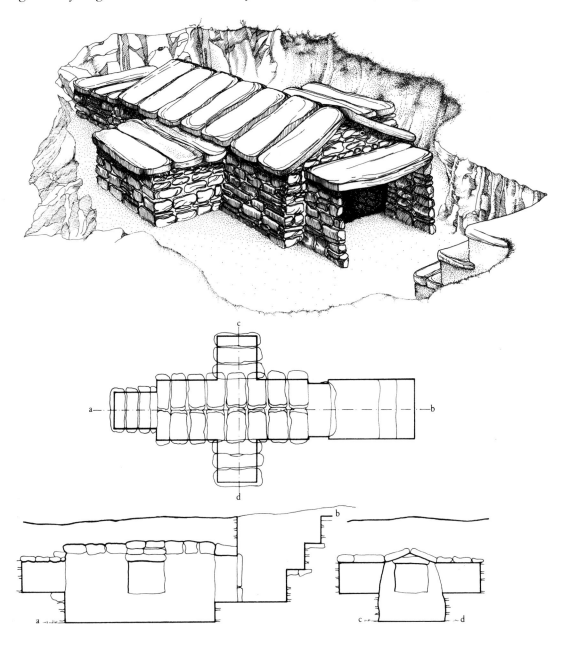

58. Reconstruction, plan, and sections of Tomb 118 at Monte Albán. Phase II (redrawn after Marquina, 1990).

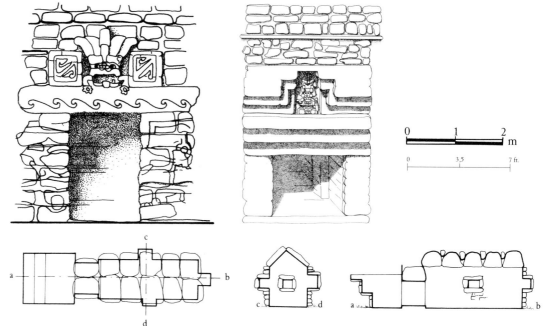

59. Façade of Tomb 50 (left) phase IIIB-IV, and of Tomb 104 (right) phase IIIA-IIIB. Bottom: plan and sections of Tomb 128 phase IIIA. Monte Albán (redrawn after Marquina, 1990).

have the entrance in the south prospect. Other important tombs of phase III are Tombs 6 and 11 at Lambityeco.

During Monte Albán IV[20] major changes swept through the entire Oaxaca region. With the fall of Teotihuacán, an overhaul of the political and economic organization of Monte Albán was necessary. Archaeological evidence tends to show that most of the population left the town, particularly the dignitaries and their families and the functionaries who gravitated round them. Consequently it is difficult to fix a precise date to these events on the basis of the tombs alone; but one of the most marked features is the return of the flat roofs, though most continued to be sloping. Orientation remained east-west, with the entrance now in the west prospect.

During Monte Albán V[21] the roofs were all flat. There are three kinds of tombs without antechambers—the rectangular type with jambs, the rectangular type with niches, and those combining both styles. The interior walls were now constructed with upside-down taludes, and the use of stucco floors became more widespread. The facades vary with the alterations to the floor plan. In the tombs

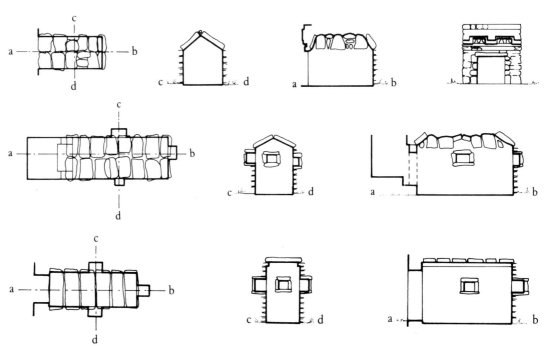

60. From top: plan, sections, and façade of Tombs 82, 84, and 86 at Monte Albán. Phase IIIB-IV (redrawn after Marquina, 1990).

106

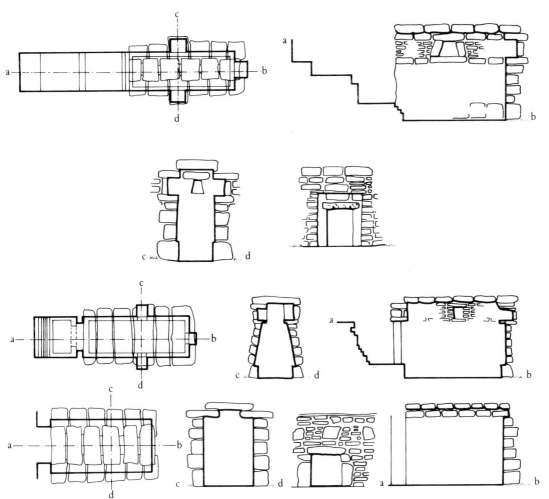

61. *From top:* plan, sections, and façade of Tombs 59, 93, and 63 at Monte Albán. Phase V (redrawn after Marquina, 1990).

without antechambers the façade is composite, whereas in those with antechambers the façade is elementary. The antechamber tombs have niches cut into the cornices.

TOMB 7

Tomb 7 is situated in System Y, a dwelling complex about 330 feet (100 meters) northeast of the Grand Plaza. This was the site of temples and large residences occupied by people of obvious high standing in Monte Albán's society, since they were buried in grand tombs beneath the floors of their homes.

Tomb 7 is constructed according to the Zapotec architectural standards of phase IIIB, and comprises two chambers set along an east-west axis, separated by two pillars. The antechamber is roofed with large horizontal slabs; the rectangular mortuary chamber is covered with sloping slabs and has a niche in the end wall. It originally contained a Zapotec burial, and the entrance was sealed with a stone engraved with typical Zapotec glyphs. The layer of earth piled against the entrance was found to contain Zapotec urns.

In phase V the tomb was reutilized by the Mixtecs, who deposited one of the richest hoards of grave goods found at Monte Albán, together with nine skeletons, all probably secondary (i.e., transferred from their original location). The main skeleton, that of a male approximately fifty-five years old, showed artificial skull deformation and filed teeth. To enter the tomb the Mixtecs removed one of the roof slabs and extracted the Zapotec material inside, but overlooked a number of objects. Once they had sealed the original entrance with earth and raised the floor level, they proceeded to scatter the tomb floor with the skeletons, jewelry, and other items of their *caciques,* or dignitaries. Finally they left by the roof, closing the aperture with the glyph-engraved slab which the Zapotecs had formerly used to bar the entrance.

As a result of these operations, the architectural features of Tomb 7, the traces of mural painting, and the objects found on the floor are all Zapotec, whereas the objects found nearer the surface belong to a later Mixtec burial, in accordance with figurations in the codices and other expressions of Mixtec culture.

TOMB 104

Tomb 104 is located outside the Grand Plaza toward the northwest, beneath the west room of a house composed of three narrow rooms around a courtyard. Inside the tomb, which dates from the transitional phase IIIA-IIIB, an adult male skeleton was found, probably that of a leading priest or important governor, laid in a supine position with a profusion of pottery, perfume jars, pots, and other small vessels. At the entrance to the mortuary chamber stood an urn depicting the rain god Cocijo, surrounded by four other smaller urns featuring the rain god's assistants, called *colanijes* in Zapotec and *acompañantes* in Spanish.

The tomb's outer façade is most elaborate: at the center of the *tablero* molding (typical of phase IIIA) is a niche containing an urn; the figure adorning it is wearing an ornate piece of headgear of plumes with the head of the god Cocijo in the middle and a jaguar head on either side; the figure is also wearing earrings and a large breastplate with shells; in his left hand he carries a receptacle for the *copal,* an aromatic resin used as incense. The figure is seated on a pedestal embellished with the head of a jaguar.

The door of the tomb consists of a massive rectangular slab engraved on both sides. The engraving on the inside was done when the tomb was built, but the

62. Urn decorating outer façade of Tomb 104 at Monte Albán.

108

outer decoration was completed later; the door was therefore reused and engraved a second time. The inner face shows a set of glyph motifs that also appear in the murals on the walls of the mortuary chamber. On the right of the door is the glyph representing the date 6 Turquoise and a small stone figure. On the left is the glyph for the date 7 Deer and 1 Serpent. In the central band there is a footprint above the abbreviate symbol for "sky" and, toward the right, the glyph 5 Turquoise.

The mortuary chamber has five niches, two in the side walls and three in the end wall (one central and two in the corners). Four of these niches contained pottery offerings.

The entire interior of the chamber is painted. The outlines of the figures were first sketched out on the stucco walls with diluted red pigment, and then filled in with various colors, each contoured with white.

Starting from the south wall (left of the entrance) a male figure is seen with a vessel in one hand and the other hand outstretched, wearing an unusual pointed headdress of plumes. Above the niche is a *caja,* or rectangular casket, painted red, white, and green surmounted by a yellow parrot. There follow two glyphs and various numerals.

On the east wall (at the end of the tomb), associated with the central niche is the glyph 5 Turquoise (the same one engraved on the inside of the door). Still in the center is a set of "Jaws of Heaven" surmounted by the "Nostrils of the Jaguar." The central face is a frontal representation of the suffix 5.

63. Reconstruction of the mortuary chamber of Tomb 104 at Monte Albán with its original contents. MNA. On the threshold stands an urn depicting a deity, accompanied by four smaller *colanijes* or "helper" urns; behind them lies the skeleton of the deceased and numerous offerings in terra cotta, both on the floor and in the niches.

64. Panoramic reconstruction of the murals decorating the three inside walls of Tomb 4 at Monte Albán.

On the north wall (on the right of the entrance) is the calendrical name 5 Owl, below which runs the name 5 Thunder (or perhaps 7 Thunder) in the form of a head. Above the niche is the name 1 Serpent, matching the one engraved on the inside of the door. And finally there is another male figure wearing an elaborate headdress in the form of a serpent's head with forked tongue. This figure is also carrying something in his left hand and has his right hand outstretched.

The two human figures in Tomb 104 are seen in profile, turned toward the back wall. These may be the ancestors of the person buried in the tomb. Of special interest are the glyphs of the year 5 Turquoise and the name 1 Serpent: they are the only known case of a tomb in which the glyphs engraved on the door reappear in the murals.[22]

TOMB 105

Tomb 105 is situated in the locality known as El Plumaje, an elongated hill running north-south, roughly 1,600 feet (500 meters) northeast of the Grand Plaza. The tomb lies beneath the residence of an important dignitary, a building that typifies the classic "small palace," or *quehui,* composed of four main rooms around a large square courtyard, with four small courts at the corners. The entrance portico, in the room on the west side of the house, was composed of two pillars supporting a massive lintel.

During excavations at the center of the main courtyard, a rectangular cavity with neatly squared-off sides and its base in rock yielded a *caja,* for funeral offerings, similar to those found beneath the corners of the South Platform; there was also an offering, comprising vases in Monte Albán III-style (very similar to the *floreros* of Teotihuacán), together with some rectangular vases, small pots and vessels, and an obsidian spoon.

Excavations beneath the east room revealed a large cruciform tomb, dated to phase IIIA, partly dug straight out of the rock. The flat roofing was made of enormous slabs. The small antechamber is reached via a set of four steps and the entrance was found blocked with oblong stones. The threshold is very low, though once inside it is possible to stand upright (the ceiling is 6.5 feet (2 meters) high). Two column fragments were found inside, together with an incomplete human skeleton and various worked animal bones; otherwise the tomb was practically empty.

The walls of the antechamber and mortuary chamber are clad in stucco and entirely embellished with murals depicting nine pairs of men and women, all in profile, presumably related to the deceased.

The first couple appears on the south doorjamb of the antechamber. The man, whose name is 2 Jaguar, is old and wears a large turban-type headdress of jaguar pelt. The woman, 1 Deer, sports a complicated headdress. The north doorjamb also depicts a couple, though rather deteriorated.

Inside the mortuary chamber on the two side walls (north and south) between the entrance and the side niches one can see a procession of couples, two on either side, proceeding toward the entrance; above them appears the sign representing the "Jaws of Heaven." The men depicted on the north wall have very similar names, composed of a merger of the glyph J and the glyph E. Each man holds a spear in his right hand, and in his left a kind of bag. Like their male counterparts, the women wear elaborate headgear, each differing from the other; their name-glyphs are also different. The men are shod in sandals, the women are barefoot. On the south wall, starting from the entrance, the sequence of figures is as follows: 3 Monkey (male), 4 Jaguar (female), 4 Serpent (male), and 12 Monkey with serpent's tongue (female). As with those on the opposite wall, each of the figures wears a bulky headdress, and each one is associated with a glyph representing his or her name. On the right hand the men are each carrying a bag. The man indicated as 3 Monkey appears to be a kind of god, scattering seeds with his left hand, similar to the priests in the murals at Teotihuacán.

Beyond the niches on either side appears another couple, moving toward the large central glyph in the back wall. This wall is also painted with a couple, the man on the left, the woman on the right. The glyph spells out "13 Death."

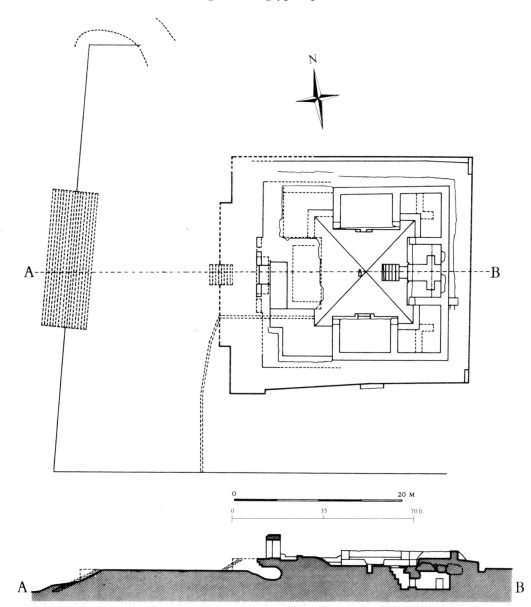

65. Plan and section of the residential complex containing Tomb 105 at Monte Albán (from Kubler, 1984).

111

66. 67. Reconstruction of the murals on the north wall *(this page)* and on the south wall *(opposite page)* of the mortuary chamber of Tomb 105 at Monte Albán (redrawn after Marquina, 1990).

The tomb's ceiling is painted red with black zones, both colors associated with funerary symbolism.

These princely tombs and their murals, dating from Monte Albán III, are open to various interpretations. The majority of skeletons found in the cruciform tombs (in equal proportion of male to female) suggest that in many cases the remains not only belong to governors, but to other members of the nobility bound in matrimony, or various members of the royal family.

The "Jaws of Heaven," which first appear during phase IIIA, are the hallmark of the royal genealogy: the fact that men *and* women in the murals in Tomb 105 are found beneath this sign suggests that descent in Zapotec customs was bilineal, as it was in the Zapotecs of the sixteenth century. This possibility is endorsed by the frequent appearance of couples in murals. The iconographic content of these murals prefigures that used in the later, Mixtec codices, in which the genealogy of the governors is represented by a series of ancestors of both sexes, and nearly always in couples.[23]

Tomb 125 is also important. This tomb, which is situated toward the northern end of the site, was built beneath the courtyard of a wealthy subject, and offers a rather original association between the façade painting and the serpent sculpture set into the wall above the lintel of the entrance to the main chamber. The tomb, with its rectangular plan, is aligned toward the south, and corresponds to phase IIIB-IV.

68. Lápida 3 with two couples from the royal dynasty; above them is the "Jaws of Heaven" symbol. From Cuilapan. Monte Albán IV. MNA.

The Population of Monte Albán through Its Tombs and Burials

The skeletons found in the tombs, as with those from simple pits in the residential sectors and other sites, offer clues to some of the physical characteristics of the ancient inhabitants of Monte Albán—the biological ages of the individuals at the time of death, their sexes and heights, the shapes of their skulls and other details of their proportions. They also tell us about specific aspects of the culture, such as the deliberate deformation of the skull and the filing or incrustation of

teeth. The analysis of the skeletal remains also enables us to identify the kinds of disease or infirmity from which these people suffered, caused by infections or malnutrition.

By comparing data from the burials with the specific features of the tombs, it is possible to attempt conclusions about the extent of stratification in the society.

During some archaeological phases in Monte Albán, the tombs outnumbered the more straightforward burials. Of the total number of interments excavated at Monte Albán, the particular phase of 42 tombs and 217 burials was not identifiable.

Percentage of Tombs and Burials at Monte Albán					
TOMBS (total 180)			BURIALS (total 325)		
Phase	Number	%	Phase	Number	%
I	8	5.8	I	11	10.8
II	22	15.9	II	14	12.9
II-III	6	4.3	II-III	3	2.7
III-A	21	15.2	IIIA	13	12.0
IIIB	33	23.9	IIIB	23	21.3
IV	41	29.7	IV	27	25.0
V	7	5.0	V	17	15.7
	138	100.0		108	100.0

(*Source:* Romero, 1983: 94)

It is generally believed that the skeletons in those tombs with rich grave goods belong to a higher social class, and the simple burials to the lower classes. But the distinction may instead correspond to the evolution of burial rites rather than to socioeconomic factors.

The burials may be classified as primary or secondary. Sixty-eight percent of the skeletons in both graves and tombs at Monte Albán are primary, that is, the skeleton retained some anatomical link, either generally or partially. The remaining burials are all secondary.

In the course of the seven archaeological phases, 71 percent of the corpses were deposited directly in the earth, 22.35 percent in a grave, and 5.88 percent in ollas, or large, bulging vessels.

Studies of the more recently analyzed material have revealed that in the tombs the male skeletons total 66 percent, and female 33 percent; whereas for the graves, the figures are 60 percent male and 40 percent female. From this one assumes that the tombs were more frequently used for burying adult males. Consequently, those in the tombs are probably the bodies of Monte Albán's governors or ruling elite.

The ages of the skeletons vary considerably between tombs and graves: in the tombs only 16 percent of the skeletons are juvenile, while in the graves the figure reaches 32 percent. This exclusion of children, youths, and women (though to a lesser extent) from the tombs, and the prevalence of adults over forty years of age would tend to suggest that, in time, an individual could improve his or her social status.

Grave goods tend to be placed at any one of our precise points beside the skeleton: near the skull, above the skull, near the pelvis, near the feet. In some cases the positions are mixed: near the skull and the feet, or near the skull and the knees.

Dental Filing, Skull Deformation, and Surgical Skull Cutting

Among the customs of the early inhabitants of Monte Albán was the practice of dental filing, which involved cutting down the teeth. It began in Monte Albán I and continued through phase V. This was accompanied by the practice of fitting studs of jade or hematite into the front teeth; this began in phase II and became most widespread in phase IV, but disappeared in phase V.

The custom of skull deformation was common throughout pre-Hispanic America and strictly observed in Monte Albán. The origin and purpose of the practice have been discussed at length. Opinions vary—some believe it was for practical purposes (to make it easier to carry heavy loads), or for reasons of personal beauty, as a prophylactic, for social status, or as a sign of ferocity; it has even been considered that the passivity or aggressivity of an individual might have depended on the amount of pressure exerted on different areas of the brain.

Scholars generally consider the practice a primarily cultural matter, a tendency for human groups to accentuate existing skull forms. But all recognize that the reasons which prompted this practice were social, and varied from group to group over the course of time.

Our knowledge of the techniques used in skull deformation stems from a variety of sources—the reports of early chroniclers, the descriptions by anthropologists, ethnological studies on contemporary peoples who still practice skull deformation, and the remains of the equipment actually used to perform the operation.

Deformation was achieved through the application of bandages, pieces of padded wood, or with special devices; these were applied to the skull during the first months of life. The final shape depended on the way the bandages were applied, varying the direction of the compression.

According to specialists, there were two kinds of deformation: tabular and annular. Tabular deformation could be oblique (by applying the pressure between the forehead and eyes), or erect (by applying the pressure between the forehead and the lambdoidal suture). Annular deformation was effected by circular compression. At

Monte Albán, skull deformation of the erect tabular type appeared in the transitional phase II-IIIA, and oblique tabular deformation in phase IIIA. From then on the two forms developed in parallel.

Ten of the skulls of the skeletons found at Monte Albán had undergone some kind of trephining, a surgical operation in which disks of bone are removed from the skull. Surgical operations on the skull are not found elsewhere in the pre-Hispanic Mesoamerica, and this makes Monte Albán unique in this practice. In a few cases, it is even possible to follow the various stages of the technique adopted. The regeneration of the bone is proof that the patient survived the operation. Trephining was only practiced during phase IIIB. Five adults with trephined skulls were found buried in houses dating from this phase.

The operation was carried out with a hollow drill that left a round hole—like the drill used in fashioning jewels and for drilling teeth for studs. It is now known whether this technique was used elsewhere in the ancient world. An alternative method was to file or cut into the skull.

In 1973 excavations in a house yielded four skeletons, male and female, laid supine, all with trephined skulls; two of them were young, but the other two were over forty years old, their skulls covered with an upturned vase. All those excavated in 1972-73 were found in graves covered with stone slabs, with no grave goods or with some domestic pottery wares. The graves were situated beneath the floors of modest dwellings. Hence the patients who underwent drilling were most likely from

69. Small terra cotta urn of a female figure showing dental filing; she is wearing a typical *quezquemitl* or short cape, and a *huipil* or long skirt. From Monte Albán. Monte Albán IIIB. MNA.

115

70. Large multicolored terra cotta urn of a male figure in which the tabular skull deformation is visible; he is wearing the bulky headdress of a broad-billed bird deity. From Tomb 77 at Monte Albán. Monte Albán II. MNA.

the lower strata of society. All the individuals with trephined skulls in Monte Albán were adult: four men and six women.

The examples of skull surgery in Europe and South America indicate that drilling was done for therapeutic reasons, usually as a remedy for skull fractures. Ethnographic studies on contemporary peoples seem to indicate that the operation was effected as a cure for brain trauma. And yet the samples that have come to light suggest that reasons for the operation varied, as there are no apparent signs of fracture, and for some reason more women were operated on than men.

Furthermore, the fact that four of the skeletons, both young and adult, were found in the same site seems to demonstrate that the practice was not entirely therapeutic. Four of the skulls with the same type of deformation showed drilling with the same technique, in the same point of the skull. Hence we might infer that the surgery was carried out for ritual rather than curative reasons.

The outcome of trephining was not always positive or pleasant: only two individuals documented survived any length of time. Although one lived long enough to undergo five separate operations, most of the patients died shortly after being operated upon. Those that survived the first attempt were generally submitted to further

71. Two of the four skeletons found in 1973 at Monte Albán in a quadruple grave beneath a commoner's dwelling dating from phase IIIB. All the individuals had been subjected to surgical skull cutting and their heads were covered by inverted bowls.

intervention, which killed them or caused imminent death. These facts suggest that the surgery was still in its experimental stages, which would explain why they continued trying until the death of the patient.

Physical Characteristics of the Inhabitants of the Central Valleys

Little is known of the physical characteristics of the inhabitants of the Valley of Oaxaca. The most extensively analyzed bone remains are those from Monte Albán, on which osteometric studies (those based on measurement of bones) have been made. But it is not always easy to establish to what period human remains belong, either because the tombs were reused, or because of the looting that often has taken place. Further complications arise due to the deterioration of the bones themselves and the considerable span of time in which the site was inhabited, during which there may have been an influx of other ethnic groups to Monte Albán.

The ancient population of Monte Albán was shorter in stature than other Mesoamerican groups; the average height for women was 4 feet, 10 inches (1 meter, 47 centimeters), and for men 5 feet, 3 inches (1 meter, 60 centimeters). It seems as if they had wide heads with the face set low or centrally.

It is thought that Monte Albán was originally occupied by a group very similar to today's population, and that many physical characteristics have been preserved over time with little change.

As noted above, physical characteristics, sex, and age also give clues to the economic and political aspects and the social stratification at Monte Albán. However, there are no significant differences between the skeletons discovered in the tombs and those found in simple graves. The physical traits of both groups are similar,

72. Terra cotta urn of an individual with typical Zapotec features.

73. Terra cotta urn of the god Cocijo seated. Monte Albán IIIB. MRO.

74. Terra cotta urn of a standing opossum-headed figure. Region of Oaxaca. Monte Albán IV. MRO.

from which we may infer that the Zapotecs were a single people in the biological sense. The discrepancies of sex and age between the two types of burial most likely stem from matters of social distinction and cultural habits.

Religion

Cult worship is a fundamental element of ancient Oaxaca, and can be traced back to the dawn of the first farming villages in which the evolving religious ceremony took on increasing importance. As the village communities expanded and their social organization grew more complex, religion became an ever increasing focus until it more or less permeated all aspects of daily life, affecting the community's sense of play, war, and trade.

The Zapotecs adored one god in particular, the creator, supreme over all other gods. He was called by different names—Coqui-Xee, Coqui-Cilla, or Pije-Tao—and was considered eternal—"uncreated, without beginning or end." He was also the overlord of the thirteen deities, or god Thirteen, associated with the thirteen sets of twenty into which the ritual calendar was divided.

Together with this god, though inferior to him, there were other gods with concrete attributes: Copichja, god of both the sun and war, and Cocijo, god of lightning, thunder, and rain. Cocijo was among the most important figures in the Zapotec pantheon, and appears in other Mesoamerican cultures. Cozaana and Nohuichana, god and goddess of men and animals, were also the protectors of ancestors. Pitao Cozobi, god of maize, recurs often in Zapotec imagery owing to the vital importance of farming to pre-Hispanic Zapotec communities. From an archaeological point of view Pitao Cozobi is linked to the bat god, the god of the glyph "L," and the god with the "monkey on his headdress." There were also other gods, such as Pitao-Xoo, god of earthquakes, Pitao-Xicala or Pecala, god of dreams, love, and luxury; Coqui-Bezelao and Xonoxi-Quecuya, god and goddess of death and the underworld. Quiabelagayo or Quie-Beloo-Gaayo, venerated in the region of Macuilxóchitl (near the site of Dainzú in the Tlacolula Valley), is represented by the name 5 Flower, a local version of the god of love.

The entire Zapotec universe was organized around a ritual calendar of 260 days. They believed that the gods controlled the flow of time and events, and that these were all divine manifestations.

In Zapotec society, each newborn was given a calendrical name, nearly always linked to some animal (an owl, lizard, deer, jaguar, bat) or to some aspect of the plant world or natural phenomena (reeds, flowers, turquoise), or even to a force of nature (wind, fire, rain, sun, earthquake). They believed that the attributes of the name were transmitted to the bearer.

In this world, in which religion and the gods were of enormous importance, there was copious production of highly refined and detailed cylindrical terra cotta vessels each with a frontal figure. On these vessels, or urns as they are generally termed, the Zapotecs molded human images of their gods, or priests with the same attributes as the gods, and—though more rarely—other illustrious figures whom the Zapotecs revered. Most of these figures are seated, sometimes cross-legged, their hands resting on their knees. The details of the hands and feet are generally simplified, while the facial features, masks, and headdresses or other symbolic elements, are sculpted with the utmost care.

Most of the urns are found at the tomb entrance or further inside, and are therefore considered funerary urns (though some have turned up in the temples or set into the facades of the tombs, where they were covered with a layer of earth).

118

Generally speaking, however, in Zapotec funerary structures the urn is clearly supposed to be part of the entrance to the tomb, as if protecting the deceased. Usually, the main urn is surrounded by a set of five or eight smaller vessels, like assistants, or *colanijes.*

Archaeological finds have corroborated the historical and ethnographic indications that besides the tombs caverns were also used for cult activity, sacrifices, and burials. The Zapotec jaguar god, symbol of power and dominion and hence a frequent icon in Monte Albán, was also associated with the god of the earth and the caverns, known as "the heart of the realm," or "the heart of the place," where propitiatory rites were held. The chosen cavern was filled with stone images of the relevant deities, in whose honor wild chickens and cockerels were sacrificed and copal incense burned. Traces of human burials have been found in caverns, as well. It seems as if a bed of sorts was prepared with *zacate,* or grass, on which the body was laid, dressed in the person's finest clothes, and wound in a mat of palm-leaves; the body was then covered with earth. Offerings were often set down beside the body—some of them were personal belongings, such as weapons, jewelry, ornaments, and pottery containing the necessary food to nourish the decreased on the journey to the afterlife. Other gifts were stone or pottery images of the gods or priests who were to protect the spirit of the deceased. The offering was put together with great care, and nothing was overlooked so as to avoid incurring the wrath of the deceased and his subsequent vendetta on his relatives.

Zapotec Art

Before we begin describing what is definable as Zapotec art, it is first necessary to bear in mind that modern aesthetics are utterly different from the artistic values expressed by Zapotec culture at its peak.

While the artistic quality, the creative power, and the aesthetic value of many pre-Hispanic works are beyond discussion, there are some who question the use of the

75. Terra cotta head of the bat god Murciélago. From Jalieza. Monte Albán IV. MNA.

76. Terra cotta vessel with the head of a broad-billed bird deity. From Zegache. Monte Albán I. MNA.

77. Detail of a stone lintel with bas-relief of a figure holding a *copal* bag in one hand. From Monte Albán. Monte Albán IIIB. MNA.

51. Terra cotta urn with the head of the god with a broadbilled bird mask. The headdress bears an unidentified glyph in association with number 13 formed with two bars and three dots. From Temple 7 Venado at Monte Albán. Monte Albán I. Museo Nacional de Antropología, Mexico City (hereafter referred to as MNA).

78. 79. Top: terra cotta brazier with an effigy of the full-lipped Young God of Fire. From Monte Albán. Monte Albán I. MNA. *Bottom:* terra cotta tripod vessel painted using fresco technique, with breast-shaped supports. It shows the influence of the Maya from Chiapas and Guatemala. From Monte Albán. Monte Albán II. MNA.

term "art" in connection with these works because, in most cases, the artifacts were not the fruit of a contemplative act, but were made with a concrete social purpose or function in mind. The pre-Hispanic cultures, which were founded on farming societies wholly dependent on nature and the elements, channeled many of their fears and apprehensions into creating objects which resembled what they saw around them. More ambitiously, other objects aimed to signify physical phenomena such as the rain, thunder, or sunlight—phenomena which in the course of time came to be revered as gods.

History has shown that things which were of enormous importance in the past can lose all meaning for the modern world. By the same token, objects and artifacts belonging to a particular outlook and philosophy may be quite worthless to others. This is particularly true in the case of the pre-Columbian civilizations: although the Spanish assimilated some aspects of the indigenous cultures they encountered in Mesoamerica, much of the accumulated knowledge of the ancient peoples was lost forever, leaving modern archaeologists the arduous task of bringing fragments of that lost universe back to light.

Today we lack the necessary keys to reading what is written on the stone stelae or in the codices, and it is extremely difficult to fathom the roles played by each of the deities, or identify each one's specific attributes. Nor can we grasp the meaning behind some of the customs and cultural models that have reached us in the form of archaeological relics.

The astonishing material legacy of these cultures which, though not entirely extinct, has been profoundly transformed, evokes amazement and admiration. As noted earlier, the aesthetic judgment given to pre-Hispanic works today, or the value attached to them, is based not only on their possible original meaning, but also on what they represent for us today, as well as on their conception and form, on the material used, and on the workmanship and results achieved. These factors combined are what we call a "work of art," and the Zapotec and Mixtec cultures of the region of Oaxaca have left many such examples.

ZAPOTEC CULTURAL TRADITION

The region of Oaxaca is situated in the center of Mesoamerica, and hence much of Zapotec civilization developed in close relation to the neighboring cultures of the Olmec, Maya, Teotihuacán, Mixtecs, and Aztecs. All these peoples spoke a language belonging to the Otomanguean linguistic family.

From the Olmec, the Zapotecs inherited several characteristic features including their system of numbering and the Olmec iconography with its jaguars and full-lipped people wearing helmut-like headgear.

By the time the Zapotecs were a distinguishable group both ethnically and culturally, they had felt the influence of the Maya from Chiapas and Guatemala, as corroborated by the borrowing of certain deities and decorative styles on pottery vessels.

Later, when they were at the height of their glory, the Zapotecs came under the sphere of influence of Teotihuacán. This can be seen in their architecture, in the murals inside their tombs, and in their pottery, to name the more important cases.

Generally speaking, the Zapotec civilization fed off similar, neighboring Mesoamerican cultures, and at the same time provided inspiration to others around it. As a result, the pre-Columbian civilizations on Mexican soil have more similarities than differences, though each one contains features that render it unique, and therefore worthy of separate study.

52. *Painted terra cotta brazier in the form of a temple, with Olmec-style warrior figures. The central figure is the Young God with bird helmet. From Monte Albán. Monte Albán* I. *MNA.*

53. Opposite: *Painted terra cotta urn with the god 5 F, seated, lavishly dressed, with eye mask. From Tomb 1 at Loma Larga in the Tlacolula Valley. Monte Albán* II. *MNA.*

54. *Painted terra cotta stand in the form of a human spine, with coccyx and vertebra; used as a stand for ollas and vases.* From Monte Albán. Monte Albán II. MNA.

55. Opposite: *Multicolored terra cotta urn with the head of the god 5 F with eye mask.* From Monte Albán. Monte Albán II. MNA.

Pages 126–27:

56. *Painted terra cotta funerary box with lid; all four faces are inscribed with the water glyph.* From Monte Albán. Monte Albán II. Museo Regional de Oaxaca, Convent of Santo Domingo, Oaxaca (hereafter referred to as MRO).

57. *Terra cotta urn with effigy of the rain god Cocijo, seated.* From the region of Oaxaca. Monte Albán II. MNA.

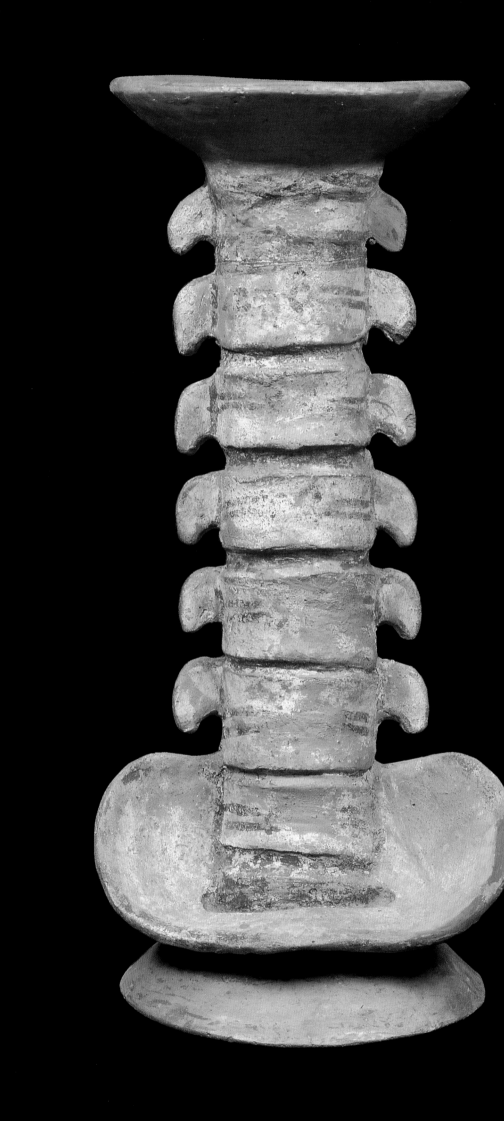

58. *Terra cotta urn with standing figure wearing jaguar headdress and elaborate breastplate. From Tomb 113 at Monte Albán. Monte Albán* II. *MNA.*

59. Opposite: *Terra cotta urn known as the Scribe Urn, featuring a seated youth wearing a headdress inscribed with the date 13 water, and 13 flint knife inscribed on breast. From Cuilapan. Monte Albán* III. *MRO.*

60. *Terra cotta urn with a standing deity in rich attire. From the region of Oaxaca. Monte Albán* IIIB-IV. *MRO.*

61. Opposite: *Terra cotta head symbolizing the dichotomy between life and death, a constant in Zapotec religious imagery. From Soyaltepec. Monte Albán* IIIA. *MNA.*

Pages 132–33.

62. *Terra cotta urn with the Old God, seated, holding out an offering of* copal, *a resin used as incense. From the region of Oaxaca. Monte Albán* IIIB-IV. *MRO.*

63. *Terra cotta urn with the Old God, seated, wearing an elaborate headdress. From the region of Oaxaca. Monte Albán* IIIB-IV. *MRO.*

64. Terra cotta urn with Xipe
Totec, an agricultural and
military deity, standing,
sumptuously dressed, and
wearing a breastplate depicting
the god Cocijo. From Tomb 51
at Monte Albán. Monte Albán
IV. MNA.

65. Opposite: Terra cotta urn
with Xipe Totec, seated. From
Monte Albán. Monte Albán IV.
MNA.

Overleaf:

66. Terra cotta urn with deity
wearing a jaguar headdress,
crowned with a second
headdress in the form of a bird
and jaguar. From the region of
Oaxaca. Monte Albán IV.
MRO.

One of the so-called principal arts is architecture. Ever since the beginnings of history, human beings have searched for food to abate their hunger, clothes to cover their bodies, and dwellings to shelter themselves. With the passage of time, dwellings gradually evolved according to the availability of building materials and climatic conditions. In many cases human beings did not only concern themselves with building their shelters, but also with giving them a "personal touch." From the unadorned caves to the most sumptuous of palaces, people have sought to distinguish their abodes from those of others.

Zapotec architecture exhibits notable extremes: on the one hand are the magnificent monumental works of the temples, plazas, ball courts, and other buildings representing the nobility and elite groups; on the other are the traditional dwellings of the peasants, constructed with the most readily available materials.

Zapotec architecture is diffuse through all the Central Valleys of Oaxaca, from San José Mogote to Monte Albán, Dainzú, Lambityeco, Huijazóo, Yagul, and Mitla, to name only the most important sites. The building characteristics changed with each epoch, but always kept a distinct Zapotec style. The frequency of earthquakes and other seismic phenomena throughout the area may account for the use of solid bases and thick walls, with flat roofs supported on cross-beams resting on columns.

At Monte Albán the influence of Teotihuacán culture is most noticeable during the Classic Period. The mighty bases are crowned with low *taludes* supporting massive *tableros.* A wide version of the Teotihuacán *alfarda* is also a frequent feature, flanking the access ramps and stairways, decorated in a similar fashion. The most characteristic element of Zapotec design lies in the *tablero,* with its double molding, known in Spanish as *tablero a doble escapulario.* The modification is splendidly effective and creates striking shadows which shift as the sun moves across the sky.

Monte Albán was destined to receive one of the most magnificent architectural complexes in the world. An ingenious layout of outstanding harmonic balance and proportion links the buildings aligned east and west of the Grand Plaza with those

80. Stone model of a Zapotec temple decorated with a *tablero a doble escapulario.*

137

81. Mitla. Exterior of the Columns Building with *tableros* grouped in threes and decorated with stepped frets in mosaic form.

dividing it in half lengthways and those bordering it on the north and south. The effect of the asymmetrical arrangement is breathtaking. It seems as if the Zapotec architects intended to make the heart of their city a visual representation of the universe as they saw it, with four cardinal points, and a central focus symbolically linking the sky with the earthly realm and with the underworld. The very site of Monte Albán at the confluence of the three valleys seems to continue this analogy on a vaster scale. As Raul F. Guerrero writes:

> if architecture is nothing more than man's subjugation of space, his dominion of the atmosphere and the natural environment, he has perfectly achieved this at Monte Albán.[24]

The Zapotec city of Mitla is another example of architecture which has been elevated to the status of art. Mitla's architects managed to interlace their buildings with wide *tableros* in sets of three, decorated with complex fret patterns called *xicalcoliuhqui*. These frets covered the entire surface of the *tablero,* making it virtually invisible to the inexpert eye. Thousands and thousands of little rectangular pieces of stone were painstakingly cut and applied to the walls. They are so remarkably well cut that each one fits perfectly, supporting the next, making the use of mortar unnecessary. Each *tablero* has its own distinct fret pattern. Originally the frets were painted white on a contrasting red background. This extraordinary workmanship has survived, virtually intact, for five hundred years.

Believing that after death one passed on to another life, the Zapotecs lavished great care on the corpses of their forebears, constructing tombs of highly diverse proportions. Among the gems of Zapotec funerary architecture are the complex tombs equipped with several antechambers in addition to the mortuary chamber proper. The exteriors of the tombs were also the object of lavish decorative work. The traditional *talud-tablero* system was enhanced with frets and mosaics (as in the tombs at Zaachila and Yagul), pottery vessels slotted into niches in the walls (Tomb 104 at Monte Albán), sculptures (Tomb 125 at Monte Albán), and huge masks in stucco featuring local personages or sacred beings (Tomb 6 at Limbityeco, and Tomb 5 at Huijazóo).

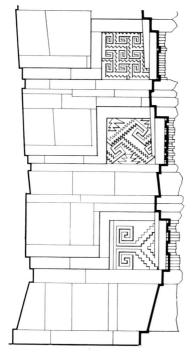

82. Detail of the *tableros* of the Columns Building at Mitla. The section shows the arrangement of small squared blocks forming the mosaic of the stepped frets (from Marquina, 1990).

138

The Zapotecs seem to have shown little interest in sculpting stone, as testified by the rarity of stelae in bas-relief, such as those at the corners of the main buildings. Instead, they achieved extraordinary skill working in terra cotta. Each of the samples found shows the hand of a master craft worker with skills handed down from generation to generation. These skills created the characteristic braziers with bat heads, vessels in the form of a jaguar's paw, containers for funeral offerings, and the miniaturized models of temples in terra cotta, each one uniquely decorated, scored, incised, modeled, and painted in one or more colors.

83. Terra cotta urn of a seated figure with folded arms, wearing elaborate ear plugs and a conical headdress. Region of Oaxaca. Monte Albán I. MNA.

From Monte Albán I (500-100 B.C.E.) a distinct Zapotec style began to emerge in the production of fabulous urns in terra cotta, roughly cylindrical in shape, with a modeled figure on the front. At first the figures were simply scored into the surface of the clay, but soon arms and legs were added. During the Classic Period (Monte Albán III), the figures became more elaborate than the vessels themselves, developing into full-fledged sculptures, some in the form of miniatures, others reaching 3 feet (1 meter) in height.

Urn production became so important that during Monte Albán IIIB some of their parts were manufactured with molds. Urns of this type have been found in all the archaeological sites, sometimes integrated with the exteriors of the tombs, but more often inside, as part of the grave goods.

With their flawlessly detailed workmanship, the urns have provided new clues to the Zapotec pantheon, on the way people dressed, the headgear they wore, and the personal ornaments that signified sex, age, and social rank. Examples of Zapotec urns are on exhibition in nearly all major museums.

LAPIDARY ART

The most powerfully evocative piece of Zapotec lapidary, or gemstone, art is a magnificent jade mask representing the god Murciélago (meaning "bat") discovered in

84. *Left:* Terra cotta vessel in the form of a jaguar's paw, with a calendrical glyph giving the year. From Monte Albán. Monte Albán IV. MNA.

85. *Right:* Terra cotta urn with the rain god seated on a pedestal. From Monte Albán IV. MRO.

86. Genealogical *lápida* featuring three different scenes. From a tomb near Cuilapan. Monte Albán IIIB-IV. MRO.

regions: the Mixteca Alta or Upper Mixteca (over 4,900 feet (1,500 meters) above sea level), the Mixteca Baja or Lower Mixteca (between 4,900 and 160 feet (1,500 and 50 meters) above sea level), and the Mixteca de la Costa or Coastal Mixteca. The first lies west of the Oaxaca Valley, and is cut through with a multitude of smaller gorges. This sub-region is in turn composed of the Mixteca Alta (*Ñuszaviuzuhu*), Chuchon Mixteca (*Tocui jñuhu,* or *Tocuijnudzyui*), which comprises a zone inhabited by groups of Chocho-Popolocas, and the Valle Mixteca (*Tocuisi ñuhu,* the Mixtec area with cultural influence from the Oaxaca valleys).

Mixteca Baja (*Ñuniñe,* or *Ñuiñe,* meaning "hot land"), lying west and northwest of the Oaxaca region, extends to the eastern border of today's Guerrero and as far as the southern part of Puebla. It is composed of lower mountains than those in the Mixteca Alta, and comprises several small valleys. The soil is more rocky and the climate more arid.

South of this lies the Mixteca de la Costa, which includes the southwest stretch of the Oaxaca lowlands. The countryside is hilly but even and relatively low yet much hotter and drier than Mixteca Baja. It is divided into two physical districts, the coastal plains and the mountain range behind them (known as *Ñuñuma* or "land of clouds").

The three main regions are also known as West, East, and South Mixteca.[1]

Language and Chronology

The Mixtec and Zapotec languages both stem from the Otomanguean family of languages. Linguistic-chronological studies carried out through the region have shown that Mixtec broke off from Zapotec somewhere around 3700 B.C.E., which also indicates that the two cultures existed at the same time.[2] This is important, because it has often been said that the Zapotecs are the oldest among the Oaxaca peoples, and the Mixtecs as a cultural group only emerged during the Postclassic Period. Although there is only one basic Mixtec language, the dialects vary from village to village; according to analysis based on words and vocabulary, the differences are directly linked to the distances between one settlement and the next. In very general terms, a dialect covers an area of approximately 37 miles (60 kilometers), that is, the distance it takes to walk in two days. Villages three days away are less likely to be visited and hence develop their own dialect; villages five days away manifest more varied dialects, and so forth.

It is nonetheless certain that first recordings of historical events—handed down in the form of pictographic documents, usually referred to as codices—date from the end of the tenth century C.E. One such codex reports of the marriage between 5 Reed Quezquémitl (blouse) of Tlaloc and her consort 9 Wind Stone Skull in the year 990 C.E. The wedding testifies to the existence of the first dynasty of Tilantongo, an important center of Mixtec power, controlling a vast region which, until the arrival of the Spanish, saw the rule of at least twenty-two generations of reigning couples. But this does not mean that the Mixtec were constituted as a cultural group only in 900 C.E.[3]

However far from having a proper chronology, Mixteca Alta has been subdivided as follows: the Lithic Period (ending around 1500 B.C.E.), the Preclassic or Village Period, with the phases Early Cruz (1500-1200 B.C.E.), Middle Cruz (1200-800 B.C.E.), and Late Cruz (800-500 B.C.E.); the Classic or Urban Period, with the phases Ramos (500 B.C.E.-300 C.E.) and Las Flores (300-800 C.E.); and the Postclassic or City-State Period, with the phases Early Natividad (800-1100 C.E.) and Late Natividad (1100-1521 C.E.).

From the archaeological explorations in the zone of Huamelulpan in the Mixteca Alta, a further chronological sequence has emerged, beginning at 400 B.C.E. and ending at 600 C.E., split into three phases: Huamelulpan I (400-100 B.C.E.), Huamelulpan II (100 B.C.E.-200 C.E.), and Huamelulpan III (200-600 C.E.).

As for Mixteca Baja, information is more scarce. Pottery classifications apply only to part of the Classic or Urban Period: phase Ñudée (500 B.C.E.-100 C.E.), undefined phase (100-300 C.E.), and phase Ñuiñe (300-800 C.E.). New data will inevitably emerge from further explorations of the region, enabling a better identification of material relative to the Preclassic and Postclassic periods.

90. Man holding a *coa,* or digging-stick, an essential tool in pre-Hispanic agriculture (redrawn after the *Codex Nuttall,* fol. 44).

Economy and Subsistence

On the basis of the archaeological material so far available, the Mixtecs, or at least their precursors, reached the area around 3000 B.C.E. Remains of hamlets in Mixteca Alta have been dated to around 1500 B.C.E.[4]

In more ancient times what is now the region of Oaxaca must have been inhabited by hunter-gatherers. Excavations have revealed an encampment set up by hunter-gatherers dating back to 2000 B.C.E., with remains of hunting weapons such as spearheads and assorted material. For the time being, it is unclear whether these groups evolved from a primitive level of subsistence to adopting farming techniques, or whether they emigrated from another area, bringing a certain level of know-how with them. More research in the area is needed, focused on this crucial early period of development.

The Mixtec people's mode of life depended on agriculture, which they had begun to practice in remote times. The most common type of settlement in the Initial and Middle Preclassic periods (1500-500 B.C.E.) was the village, which continued for a very long time. This period is also known as the Village or Formative Period. In sites such as Etlatongo and Yucuita (in the Mixteca Alta) good examples of these stages of cultural evolution have come to light. Sedentary life begins when humans learn to domesticate plants and to store surplus produce. Some authors argue that both villages enjoyed the right conditions for the transition to a sedentary culture. Their diet suggests that the inhabitants realized how to produce certain crops, including maize, beans, chili peppers, squash, and avocado, and also build suitable storage systems in which to preserve them, as proved by the discovery of storage pits.[5]

91. 92. Maize field with a sleeping man and sheaves of maize (redrawn after the *Codex Vindobonensis,* fols. 11 and 26).

The settlements were small, perched on the upper part of the hillside surrounding a rich valley fed by several streams. The Yucuita River, which runs from north to south, was the main source of water for the site of the same name, and for Coyotepec, in much the same way as happened in the Oaxaca Valley with the site of Tierras Largas.

The diet of crops was supplemented with game and fish. The ecosystem of each sub-region offered a particular resource. The lowlands offered crops of cotton and cacao, plants that would not grow in other regions, particularly on higher ground, whereas another plant, agave, grew badly in the humid climate of the highlands. Both flora and fauna therefore varied from zone to zone. The area abounded with wild game, but only dogs and turkeys were actually domesticated.

Traded products were various, and one of the most important was a powerful pigment extracted from the cactus cochineal (*Dactylopius coccus*), used for dyeing cotton a crimson color for weaving cloth. Besides the dye, exotic feathers were also widely traded for their magnificent coloring.

One of the main resources for those living along the coast was fish, which was dis-

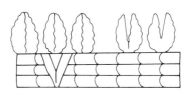

93. Cacao plants (redrawn after the *Codex Vindobonensis,* fol. 44).

147

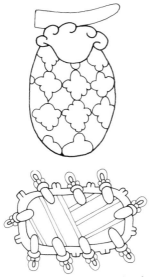

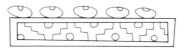

94. 95. *Pulque (top)* and jade *(bottom)* (redrawn after the *Codex Vindobonensis,* fols. 26 and 49).

96. Beans (redrawn after the *Codex Bodley,* fol. 18).

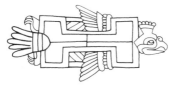

97. 98. Badger *(top)* and opossum *(bottom)* (redrawn after the *Codex Nuttall,* fols. 26 and 3).

99. Pheasant (redrawn after the *Codex Vindobonensis,* fol. 17).

tributed through the markets dried and preserved in salt. Salt was a key product of the coastal inhabitants, though it was also produced in the plateau.

Precious stones and metals were utilized by the Mixtecs themselves, but also traded with other peoples. The art of metalworking came by sea from the present-day countries of Costa Rica and Colombia around the ninth century C.E.[6]

Each region traded its own products, which flowed in all directions: cotton, clothing, cacao, fruit, vegetables, fish, salt, ornaments, and feathers were transported from the coastal and humid areas to the high valleys of the Mixteca Alta, where they were exchanged for agave fiber, *pulque* (an alcoholic beverage made from agave), maize, beans, chili peppers, metals, and precious stones. Another product may have been a form of handmade paper, and pottery from the Mixteca Alta and the north of the Mixteca Baja.[7]

During the sixteenth century throughout the Mixtec area intensive agriculture was practiced in the valleys and humid plains along the coast, providing the basis of the Mixtec economy.

Information on the diet of ancient populations can be gleaned from the fossil remains of the flora and fauna in the area they inhabited, and by studying the tools and receptacles used for the preparation and preservation of foodstuffs. Further clues are offered by analyzing the skeleton remains for indications on the health of the deceased.

Studies carried out so far suggest that, in general, the Mixtecs had the same diet as their Mesoamerican contemporaries; this was based on a combination of maize, beans, chili peppers, and squash. Maize was prepared in various ways, usually ground into a flour with a *metate*, or mortar, then mixed with water to make tortillas, tamales, and various other dishes. Maize was also an ingredient for beverages.

This staple was integrated with other wild food gathered locally, such as wild fruit, roots, leaves, pods, and walnuts, depending on what the area offered.

Most of the animal protein came from rodents, serpents, lizards, and similar animals. Turkey, deer, dog, and wild fowl were reserved for the tables of the ruling classes.[8] According to some anthropologists, as the organization of a society gradually becomes more complex, with the division of labor and the appropriation by a dominant group of the surplus produce, a negative biological relation is set up. There is a shift away from subsistence—in which there was a better distribution of food resources among the population—and a loss of the balanced diet of what was cultivated, gathered, hunted, or fished.

It has been shown that the groups of hunter-gatherers lived longer than the farming populations, and suffered from fewer diseases caused by malnutrition. In general, living conditions among hunter-gatherers were more suitable for the harmonious development of the human body than living conditions for those residing in towns and villages.[9]

Regarding the pre-Hispanic peoples who developed in what is now the state of Oaxaca, studies made on bone remains to determine diet patterns are virtually nonexistent. The knowledge we already have on the social stratification from the detailed work of paleontology and diet analysis could therefore be supplemented.[10]

One of the most reliable sources of information for assessing the living conditions and health of pre-Hispanic populations stems from the identification of some of the diseases affecting certain individuals.

Pathologies can generally be associated with certain living conditions; sometimes the critical factor is the individual's work, his or her position in the social structure, or his or her beliefs or cultural practices.

The quality of research depends largely on the quantity of bone remains belonging to the same series, and their state of preservation. If there are only a few individuals to study, conclusions are necessarily limited to certain diseases, and to their diffusion in a given area (as in the case of tuberculosis or treponematosis). It is not possible to ascertain the frequency or epidemic repercussions on the life of the group.

Certain illnesses are considered nonspecific indicators of the general state of health of a given population. Stress-related diseases are also recognized; they might be infection, undernourishment, or any other kind of ailment, without the direct cause being clear. In other cases deficiencies in diet are identified in the course of paleo-pathological studies. These include deficiency of Vitamin C, which can be detected in bones and teeth. A diet based on carbohydrates or proteins can be assessed through the analysis of certain chemical compounds that remain in bone tissue for centuries, such as strontium. The presence of kidney stones suggests a protein-rich diet, whereas scale on the teeth, together with signs of tooth decay, suggest a diet rich in carbohydrates.[11]

100. Woman named 7 Water, in a *quezquemitl* (redrawn after the *Codex Nuttall,* fol. 40).

The type, frequency, and distribution of bone fractures also give an idea of the principle kinds of physical work undertaken by the population. In other cases, the rate of growth around the articulation is studied and compared against the possible activity of the groups. Osteopathological analysis has revealed some of the more common ailments afflicting the inhabitants of the area; these include osteoarthritis, a typical disease linked to aging, and signs of infection or metabolic disorders. Anemia is frequently detected from bone remains. Its causes lie in the reduction of certain components of the blood, such as hemoglobin (the red corpuscle protein containing iron). Iron deficiency can have a genetic basis, or stem from diet imbalances, insufficient absorption, excessive demand for minerals due to a loss of blood, or to gastrointestinal infection. It does not look as if there were genetic causes for anemia among the ancient Mesoamericans, which means it must have resulted from diet deficiencies and from the inability to absorb iron due to infections of the intestinal tract.

101. Man named 9 Rabbit, in a breechcloth (redrawn after the *Codex Nuttall,* fol. 57).

The typical costume of the ancient Mixtecs was similar to clothing worn throughout Mesoamerica. Women wore a *quezquemitl* (a sleeveless blouse) and a *huipil* (a long skirt). Men wore a breechcloth, a cape around their shoulders, and an agave or cotton blanket. Clothes varied in pattern and coloring, according to region and social status. The chieftains, priests, and nobles wore the most lavish and elaborate apparel. For ceremonies they donned special attire of dazzling colors and fabulous plumed decorations.

Ornaments and jewelry were widely used—bracelets, armlets, necklaces, rings, diadems, earrings, and all kinds of other embellishments were employed to enliven the appearance. An extraordinary example of this can be seen in the Mixtec offering in Tomb 7 at Monte Albán.[12]

Social Organization

The Mixtec region was densely populated. Some authors estimate that when the conquistadores arrived there were about 1,056,000 inhabitants.[13]

It is thought that the basis of the early village societies was the family, which was composed of what we call today the "nuclear family," i.e., mother, father, and children, usually with five members.

The domestic unit has been identified by archaeologists as being composed of a house, storage pits, ovens, refuse pits, and the skeletons of preceding occupants who were buried beneath the floor inside the house or just outside.

102. Figure named 10 Flint, in a cape decorated with feathers (redrawn after the *Codex Nuttall,* fol. 56).

The first villages comprised between three and ten domestic or family units. Unlike what takes place in today's villages, during this period the villages were grouped in clusters, termed "nucleated" because of their closeness to one another. This means that there existed a unity between groups or communities. The families were held together by marriage bonds or blood ties, and each village formed a unique entity distinct from the others.

In the earliest times there was no clear social or economic distinction, which implies that everyone related on an equal basis. But work was specialized—some wove cloth, some made pottery, others built, hunted, or engaged in fishing or farming. The entire community related directly to its natural surroundings, a contact that determined the emergence of the main deities.

At the start of the Classic or Urban Period (Ramos phase, 500 B.C.E.-300 C.E.), the Mixtec social model still largely revolved around the family unit, but the divi-

103. Multicolored terra cotta vessel in the form of an old man with a jar on his back. Region of Oaxaca. Monte Albán III. MRO.

sion of labor had become more complex. More individuals began to specialize and production was increasingly varied. Meanwhile, an administrative elite with adjutants emerged, acting as mediators between the domestic units and the community as a whole. As yet there was no supreme head, but the elite were steered by a council of elders representing the most prominent families in each village or neighborhood.[14]

The Mixtec region has not yet yielded signs of an extensive state organization or other social or political control like those found in large urban centers such as Teotihuacán, Tenochtitlán, Tikal, and Monte Albán. Despite this, the region had large communities, such as Cerro de las Minas, Huamelulpan, Yucuita, and Yucuñudahui toward the end of the Classic or Urban Period (Las Flores phase, 300-800 C.E.).

It is supposed that there were other urban centers of varying importance, divided into neighborhoods, each one superintended by one of its more distinguished families.

During the Classic or Urban Period, the society was split into two opposing classes, with the closed circle of the aristocracy on one side and the main body of the people on the other. The aristocracy itself was divided between the governing class and the nobles (*tay toho*), who acted as administrators, assistants, or supervisors. They also owned slaves and retained the right to exact tributes and services from members of the population assigned to them. The bulk of society was made up of the common people (*ñanday tayñuu, tayycuo,* or *tay sicaquai*)—farmers, traders, crafts workers, peasants with farm plots, servants, and slaves (*tay situndayu*). The slave group was divided into prisoners of war made to serve as slaves (*tay nicuvainduq*), born slaves (*dzayadzna*), and slaves that could be bought and sold (*dahasaha,* or *tayñohoyahui*) as tax. These individuals could also be sacrificed during the festivals.[15] People engaged in trading had a vital role in the daily life of the community.

Although there is no evidence of a distinct social class for the military, it may well have existed. As in other corners of the world, and throughout the entire history of humankind, most armies were composed of the populace. In the case of the Mixtecs the soldiers were peasants and commoners, who, when the need arose, were forced to drop their tools and take up arms. From what may be gathered from the codices, in the Postclassic or City-State Period (800-1521 C.E.), there was definitely a class of governor-soldiers, or soldier-governors, or simply soldiers who, though not necessarily of noble lineage, distinguished themselves in battle and won recognition and distinction for themselves in the social hierarchy. These military chiefs, besides deciding the course of action in military matters, were in a position to form alliances through marriage or commercial exchange for personal benefit; alternatively they could undertake military campaigns against other groups that resisted Mixtec expansionism. All this enabled officers to better their position and secure themselves economic rewards.

Given the geographic characteristics of the Mixtec region, though they shared a culture, language, and religion, the various *cacicazgos* (local communities) were for-

104. The military chief and ruler of Tilantongo named 8 Deer Jaguar Claw, and glyphs of the places he conquered in the year 7 Flint (redrawn after the *Codex Nuttall,* fol. 43).

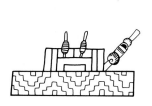
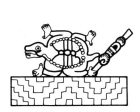

105. Noblewoman named 9 Monkey, sister of 8 Deer (redrawn after the *Codex Nuttall,* fol. 43).

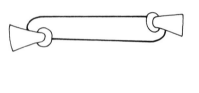

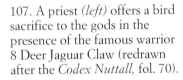

106. Burins, or flint tools, with tips in malachite and jaguar claws (redrawn after the *Codex Vindobonensis,* fol. 37).

107. A priest *(left)* offers a bird sacrifice to the gods in the presence of the famous warrior 8 Deer Jaguar Claw (redrawn after the *Codex Nuttall,* fol. 70).

Opposite page:

108. Terra cotta vessel in the form of a kneeling man with a heavy pannier, or basket-like container, on his back. From Tomb 13 at Yagul. Monte Albán v. MRO.

ever fighting for the most fertile land. This struggle is illustrated in the codices, which recount the exploits of the great soldier and leader, 8 Deer Jaguar Claw.

Priests were drawn as often from the common folk as from among the nobility. While performing specific duties separate from the rest of the population, it seems that the priesthood was not a class of its own; members were chosen at birth by the elders and received special instruction in religious matters, and were generally related to the *cacique,* or governor, of the place, who thereby reinforced his authority over the community.

Schematically, the Mixtec society resembles a pyramid with the privileged, ruling class at the top composed of the local ruler, his wife, children, and family members. Immediately below him came the more variable group of nobles, of undetermined though relatively small number. One rung below these were the majority of the *macehuales,* or people, and a lesser number of farm workers, servants, and slaves who tended the houses and lands of the governors and nobles. *Macehuales* were both workers and subjects; there may have been some kind of stratification, though there are no signs of hereditary hierarchies. Some researchers have suggested that one of the ways to move up the social ladder was to practice healing, midwifery, or the art of divination. Such individuals were all peasants of sorts, who occasionally carried out special duties.

The lowest rung of the social ladder was occupied by slaves—prisoners of war, those who sold themselves because they were unable to meet their debts, and those who were serving a penalty for having broken the laws of the community. One such example is found in the *Relación de Tecomastlahuaca:*

and those who had debts and no means to pay them, became perpetual slaves; they were engaged as servants, or sold ... or used for sacrifice, or disposed of as deemed fit.[16]

Cerro de las Minas

69. Stairway and "alfarda,"
or ramp, faced in stucco.

70. 71. Views of buildings.

72. Above: *Four pendants and a pendant ring from Tomb 7 at Monte Albán; gold worked with lost wax process and filigree. Monte Albán* V. MRO.

73. *Three pieces of gold jewelry worked with lost wax process and filigree, from Tomb 7 at Monte Albán.* Left: *Pectoral ornament in sections, depicting ball court, sun disk, flint knife symbolizing the moon, Tlatecuhtli (the monster of the earth), and rattle pendants.* Top right: *Necklace of eleven threads laced with round and oval beads and rattle pendants.* Bottom right: *Necklace with tortoiseshell and rattles. Monte Albán* V. MRO.

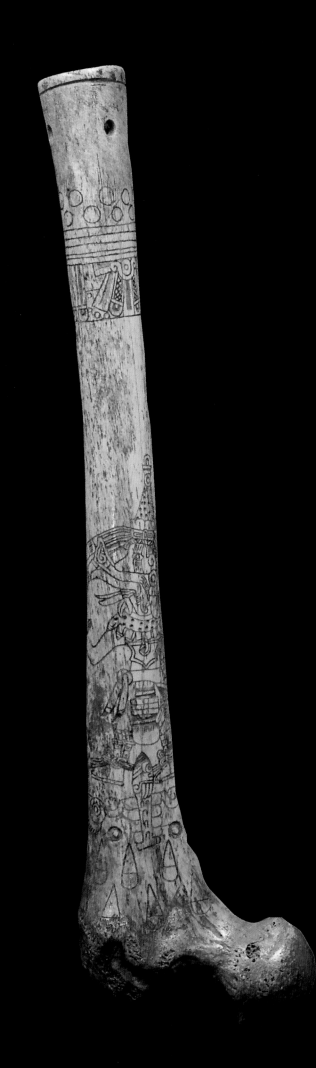

74. *Two pieces of gold jewelry worked with lost wax process and filigree, from Tomb 7 at Monte Albán. Top: Breastplate featuring a warrior with calendrical glyphs. Bottom: Pendant with the head of the god Xipe Totec. Monte Albán V. MRO.*

75. Right: *Human femur engraved with the effigy of a high priest. These bones were used as batons for command, and were suspended from a hole drilled at one end. From the region of Oaxaca. Monte Albán V. MNA.*

76. Opposite: *Human skull from Tomb 7 at Monte Albán, encrusted with pieces of turquoise, with shells for the eyes and nose. Monte Albán V. MRO.*

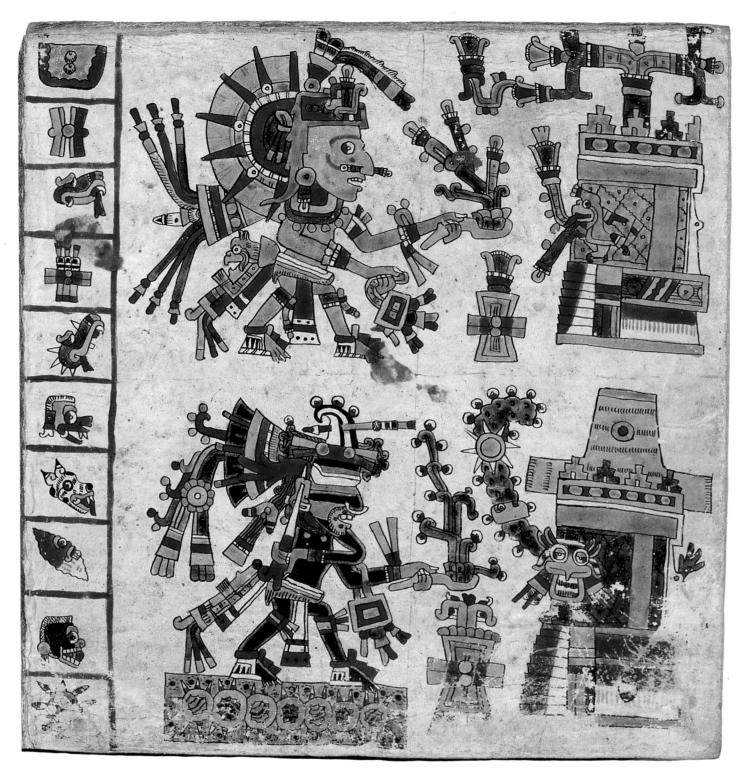

77. *Folio 12 recto, Codex Cospi, Biblioteca Universitaria, Bologna. Upper part shows the sun god Tonatiuh burning* copal *before a temple crowned with a flowering tree and a singing bird inside. Lower part shows the deity Itztlacoliuhqui-Ixquimilli, piercing his earlobe and burning* copal *before a thatched temple, out of which emerge an owl and a dark cloud. Column on left features signs of the days of the ritual calendar.*

78. Opposite: *Sheet 7 recto, Codex Cospi, Biblioteca Universitaria, Bologna. Top row: enthroned human figures with divinatory symbols. The five lower rows show a head or symbol of a deity on the left, with the twenty signs of the days of the ritual calendar of 260 days on the right. Left to right, the day signs read: dog, money, grass, reed; flint, rain, flower, crocodile; death, deer, rabbit, water; jaguar, eagle, vulture, movement; wind, house, lizard, serpent.*

79. *Multicolored terra cotta urn with the Old God seated on a pedestal decorated with stepped fret patterns, a brazier balanced on his head. From Cerro de las Minas. Monte Albán III. Ñuiñe Culture. MRO.*

80. Opposite: *Multicolored terra cotta urn in the form of a human head adorned with ear plugs and headband with a bird figure. From Zaachila. Monte Albán V. MNA.*

Pages 180–81:

81. *Ceramic whistle vessel. The warrior, armed with an atlatl, or spear-thrower, and a shield, makes a whistling sound as the water passes through the vessel. From the region of Oaxaca. Monte Albán V. MNA.*

82. *Multicolored, codex-style ceramic pitcher. From Tomb 36 at Coixtlahuaca. Monte Albán V. MRO.*

83. *Wide-necked tripod vessel in multicolored ceramic, painted with feather motifs. From the Mixteca Alta. Monte Albán V. MRO.*

84. *Wide-necked, multicolored, codex-style tripod vessel depicting a procession of priests. From the reigion of Oaxaca. Monte Albán V. MRO.*

Overleaf:

85. *Multicolored, codex-style ceramic vessel with two small handles. From the region of Oaxaca. Monte Albán V. MNA.*

Toward the tenth century C.E. the Mixtecs learned from the peoples of Central and South America how to work malleable metals such as gold, silver, and copper. Thanks to their geographic location, the Mixtecs had access to materials otherwise hard to come by, such as *tecalli* (Mexican onyx, either a banded calcite, a mediocre quality of travertine marble, or alabaster), with which they manufactured vases either in vegetal form or decorated with mythological features. Through trade, they purchased turquoise (from New Mexico and North America) and created dazzling mosaics composed of hundreds of tiny *tesserae,* which they also used to decorate the skulls of their deceased chieftains and priests. They also manufactured gold and turquoise pendants.

Alfonso Caso's landmark discovery of Tomb 7 at Monte Albán restored the marvels of Mixtec art to the world. The 300 objects found in this tomb include artifacts in semiprecious stone such as jadeite or American jade, rock-crystal (a rare material difficult to fashion), opal, obsidian, agate, and amethyst. Other finds include objects made in amber, slate, and black amber; precious delicate hieroglyphic scenes carved into jaguar or deer bone, some with turquoise inserts; objects in shell; necklaces, bracelets, anklets, pendants, and rings in river pearls, coral, shell, bone, fish vertebrae, jade, or turquoise; and delicately wrought gold figures made with the lost wax process, or with lamination or filigree technique. The Mixtecs were highly skilled goldsmiths, and even managed to fashion objects of combined gold and silver, a great achievement for those times.

One of the most remarkable finds is the so-called pendant of Yanhuitlán, a shield-shaped pendant with jade inserts, found in the Mixtec region. Other key finds include the numerous pendants from Tomb 7 at Monte Albán, with the effigies of Cocijo, the god of rain and wind; Xochilpilli-Macuilxochitl or 5 Flower, god of sexuality; Tezcatlipoca; Xipe-Totec (see color plate 74), the deity of agriculture and warfare, who is frequently depicted as a warrior priest clothed in the skin of a sacrificial victim; Tonatiuh; Quetzalcoatl, the plumed serpent; and Cuauhtemoc, or "falling eagle," among others.

Another object finely wrought in gold using the lost wax process is a breastplate

144. 145. Two vessels in *tecalli.* *Top:* tripod vessel with serpent feet, from the Mixtec region, Monte Albán V. MNA. *Bottom:* tripod olla, from Tomb 7 at Monte Albán. Monte Albán V. MRO.

146. Pendant in gold, mosaic, and turquoise. From Yanhitlán. Monte Albán V. MNA.

147. Gold breastplate with deity. From Tomb 7 at Monte Albán. Monte Albán V. MRO.

148. Two gold pendants with the flower god Xochipilli. From Tomb 7 at Monte Albán. Monte Albán V. MRO.

from Tomb 7 at Monte Albán, 4.3 inches (11 centimeters) high and weighing 3.9 ounces (112 grams) (see color plate 74). According to Caso, it represents a warrior wearing a mask in the form of a skinned mandible, or lower jaw, over his mouth, and an ample headdress bearing the effigy of the jaguar-serpent. The bust of the figure is composed of two square plaques with calendrical inscriptions: the one on the left features the Zapotec god Cocijo with ten points and a flint with two points; the right plaque bears the year glyph (resembling a capital A and O superimposed) with a house at its center and eleven points encircling it. The breastplate is thought to indicate the day "2 Flint" of the year "10 Wind" of the Zapotec calendar, which is the equivalent to the Mixtecs' year "11 House," and provides clues on correspondences between the two calendars.[32]

Another gold breastplate found in Tomb 7 at Monte Albán is particularly worthy of attention. It is composed of four linked plaques clearly inspired by the Mixtec vision of the cosmos (see color plate 73). In descending order, the first is oblong and depicts a ball court, with a deity/player at either side, holding a ball; at the center is a *marcador* in the form of the skull of Tezcatlipoca. The ball game symbolizes the struggle between two opposing divine powers: day and night, or life and death. The second plaque shows the sun-disk surrounded by a stream of blood with a skull in the center. The third plaque is a square featuring a flint knife—symbolizing the moon—complete with eyes and mouth spouting flames. The last plaque bears the image of Tlaltecuhtli, the lord of the earth, devourer of everything and eater of human bodies (leaving only their bones). The plaques are held together by rings, and from the last plaque hang four pendants composed of rosettes, plumes, spherical rattles, and lastly, teardrop-shaped rattles.

POTTERY

The Mixtecs were also highly skilled in the manufacture of multicolored ceramics. Their pottery comes in a great variety of shapes, some standard, some highly

149. 150. Two gold pendants from a tomb at Coixtlahuaca. *Left:* rattle with a serpent. *Right:* head of an old man with large ear plugs. MRO.

151. Pair of disks in gold with the sun glyph. MRO.

imaginative: tripod vases, globular vases, vases with animal-shaped feet, jars, jugs, ollas, plates, bowls, beakers, or vases in the shape of skulls, skeletons, eagles, turkeys, serpents, squashes, etc. Embellishments are either engraved or modeled, but in most cases decoration includes pigment in black, white, red, orange, pink, ocher, yellow, or turquoise hues. Each piece was finished with great care and polished after firing so that the colors glisten as if the surface had been glazed. This is how they appeared to the archaeologists who found them, centuries later. Well-known Mixtec vessels include those with painted, codex-style decorations in which the standard geometric patterns are combined with all manner of figures and symbols: plumage, ritual animals, calendrical glyphs, deities, priests, warriors, flowers, clouds, skulls, skeletons, and mythological scenes. These glimpses of history painted on Mixtec pottery are utterly fascinating, and deserve in-depth study.

Mixtec art was much admired at the end of the pre-Columbian era. When they invaded Oaxaca, the Aztecs exacted heavy tributes from the Mixtecs in the form of

152. Three terra cotta vessels painted with multicolored patterns. *Left:* tripod vessel from Yagul. *Center:* small bowl with a hummingbird from Tomb 1 at Zaachila. *Right:* tripod vessel from Monte Albán (drawings by Terry Prewitt, from Whitecotton, 1984).

153. Codex-style terra cotta tripod vessel with multicolored decoration and serpent feet. Decorated with birds and serpents. Region of Oaxaca. Monte Albán v. MNA.

gold artifacts, ceramics, greenstone, and other items, many examples of which have come to light in the course of excavation at the Templo Mayor in Tenochtitlán in Mexico City.

154. Multicolored terra cotta jaguar-claw vessel. Region of Oaxaca. Monte Albán IV. MRO.

155. Tripod scent bottle in openwork terra cotta with a handle in the form of a bird's head. Region of Oaxaca. Monte Albán IV. MNA.

When we refer to pre-Hispanic codices, we have to bear in mind the historical knowledge of the people who created them, including the Maya, the Aztecs, and the Mixtecs. These pictographic documents on native papers or deerskins folded in concertina fashion provide a great many details on the more salient aspects of the evolution of each of these peoples. Most of the codices were deliberately destroyed by Spanish missionaries such as Juan de Zumárraga and Diego de Landa. There were, however, other members of the priesthood who realized the immense value of these documents, such as Bernardino de Sahagún, Juan de Torquemada, and Francisco de Burgoa, who had this to say on the Mixtec codices:

> there are many books made from leaves or canvasses of the bark of special trees which grow in warm lands, and they tanned them and prepared them like parchment, more or less a third of a *vara* high [roughly 11 inches (28 centimeters)] and joined in a long strip as many as were necessary, on which they wrote all their histories, using characters so concise that on a single face they described a place, site, and province, year, month, and day, with all the other names of the gods, ceremonies, sacrifices, and victories.[33]

156. Mixtec origin myth and migration scene. Two divine couples *(bottom)*, sprung from the "Tree of Life" *(top right)* at Apoala, give birth to four offspring *(top)*, who then begin their journey to found the Mixtec empire (redrawn after the *Codex Nuttall,* fol. 36).

Much of what we are able to "read" on the Mixtec pre-Columbian codices is the result of the painstaking research of Alfonso Caso, who began working on them in 1932. His studies, published posthumously,[34] analyze eight codices which had al-

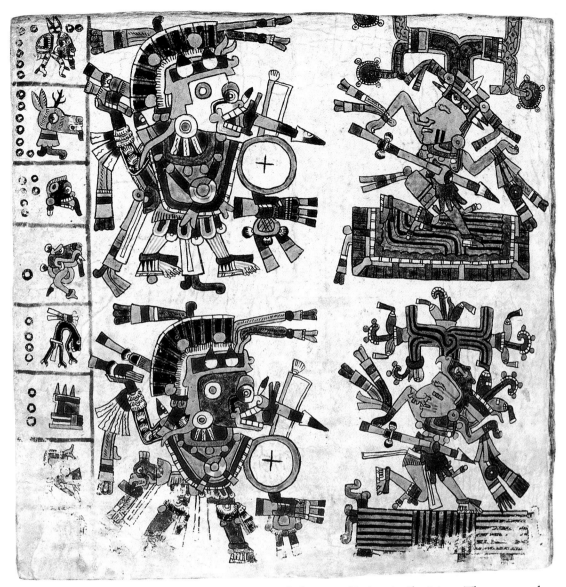

157. Scene with four deities. *Left:* two images of Tlahuizcalpantecuhtli impersonating the Morning Star, throwing his darts at the goddess of water *(top),* and the goddess of agriculture *(bottom right). Codex Cospi,* fol. 9r.

ready been grouped together because of their stylistic similarities. These are the *Becker I, Becker II, Bodley, Colombino, Nuttall, Vindobonensis,* and *Selden* codices, and the *Selden* scroll.

In the course of his studies, Caso came to three conclusions:

1) All the codices in this group are indeed Mixtec. The *Nuttall, Vindobonensis, Bodley, Colombino,* and *Becker I* codices refer specifically to the dynasties governing the Mixtec region, whereas the others are attributable to this area for stylistic reasons.

2) They were all put together immediately prior to or during the Spanish Conquest (*Nuttall and Vindobonensis* in 1438, the *Bodley* in 1519, and the *Selden* in 1456).

3) Their contents are fundamentally historical. The reverse of the *Vindobenensis,* the *Nuttall,* the *Colombino* codices, and the first part of the *Bodley* codex relate the genealogical histories of the dynasties of Tilantongo, Teozacoalco, and Tututepec. The others, which some scholars thought to be ritual, religious, or mythological books, are actually about the divine origins of the founders of the dynasties—the first kings of specific places—and the marriages between the gods, whose offspring were human.[35]

There is a second group of five pre-Columbian codices, classified by Eduard Seler[36] at the start of the 1900s and labeled the Borgia Group from the name of the most representative of the codices it contains. This group includes the *Borgia, Cospi,*

191

Féjérváry-Mayar, Laud, and *Vaticanus B 3773* codices. All center on a ritual or calendrical topic. Investigations are under way regarding their provenance, but the artistic style suggests origin somewhere in Oaxaca or Puebla, the authorship being Mixtec.

Besides the sheer beauty of these manuscripts, whose pages are authentic works of art, the Mixtec codices have enormous historical and cultural value. They provide an invaluable source of information on the geographic environment, architectural styles of temples and palaces, styles of dress, personal ornament, customs, deities, governors, subjugated cultures, sacrificial victims, and, most of all, on events, births, marriages, deaths, and so forth. This vital medium of conserving and transmitting the major historical or religious facts of each Mixtec realm is slowly being deciphered, and in future we will have a more complete knowledge of this marvelous civilization which has left a further testament to its greatness in these fabulous illuminated books.

The Mixtec Invasion of the Central Valleys

The invasion of the Central Valleys was part of a long, steady process of expansion and conquest by the Mixtecs that began in the twelfth century.

Joseph Whitecotton affirms that:

> The rise of the Mixtec states signals the beginning of the Postclassic Period in Mesoamerica and the arrival of a particular type of militaristic state based on tribute and conquest. Postclassic Mixtec society involved a transfer of political power from what were theocratic rulers to secular warlords, although their culture was built on the remnants of the Classic heritage.[37]

Although the transfer of power may not have followed this scheme of development, it is certain that the Postclassic Period was a time of overall expansion and conquest.

158. Seven different glyphs of conquered places, and the deity 9 Wind (Ehecatl-Quetzalcoatl) (redrawn after the *Codex Nuttall,* fol. 46).

159. The king on his throne receives tribute (redrawn after the *Codex Nuttall,* fol. 78).

There are several possible hypotheses. Some suggest a growth in the population that put pressure on the society's food resources, prompting a militaristic move to stem the resulting "ecological dilemma." Another suggestion is the emergence of political disagreement caused by a power vacuum upon the fall of the Classic "empires," prompting the search for new bases for political power. Others argue that expansion resulted from the struggle for new territories, or the submission of peoples through taxes.

Some scholars reason that marriage alliances were preliminary or necessary to eventual takeover, and that the Mixtecs thus managed to permeate the Valley of Oaxaca. According to the reports specific to Cuilapan and Teozapotlán in the *Relaciones Geográficas del Siglo XVI*, the Mixtecs entered the valley around 1280. That year there were two marriage alliances between people of the Mixtec dynasty and the Zapotecs. The first couple comprised a Mixtec woman and a lord from Teozapotlán (Zaachila). The second marriage saw the union of the lord's sister to a Mixtec nobleman, a few years before the arrival of the Spanish. The upshot of this union was the cession of Cuilapan to the new couple, who settled in the site, and many others of Mixtec stock followed suit.[38] The Mixtecs referred to in the *Relaciones* came from Almoloyas in the Mixteca Alta, northwest of Yanhuitlán.

After closely studying the pre-Hispanic Mixtec codices and colonial records, Alfonso Caso detected some links between the people of Cuilapan and those of Yanhuitlán. He also drew connections between the figures mentioned in the documents and the individuals represented in the tombs at Zaachila. Consequently, the codices were acknowledged as authentically historical, and therefore of the utmost importance.[39]

The *relación* on Cuilapan gives the original name of this site as Sayucu, meaning "at the foot of the hills." The Mixtecs who settled here spread their influence through the Valley of Oaxaca, and founded new villages in areas previously occupied by the Zapotecs. They also made vassals of other peoples in the area, forcing them to pay tribute. While the documents offer different versions of the facts and disagree on the dates, it is probable that all of this took place shortly before the appearance of the Spanish. Research has shown that the Mixtecs of Cuilapan expelled the Zapotec lord from Zaachila, who fled to Tehuantepec, a district he had formerly ruled.

These circumstances were part of a process of political and social organization that sought alliances through kinship with the aim of acquiring new land. Mixtec expansion in the valley therefore came about with the overthrow of the Zapotec gover-

193

nor and the seizure of his political authority. Later, the Mixtecs and Zapotecs lived side by side, in different districts, and in constant conflict.

According to Francisco de Burgoa, the lord of Zaachila sealed an alliance with the Mixtecs to conquer the Mixe and Huave populations of the Isthmus of Tehuantepec. But disagreement soon arose over the sharing of the land. Disgrunted, the Mixtecs promptly declared war on the inhabitants of Zaachila, forced them to flee, and overran their land.[40]

The centers around Cuilapan included both Mixtec and Zapotec living districts, and the inhabitants set up marriages between the two parties, creating coalitions when they were not actually at war with each other. The resulting community of tenuous, constantly changing bonds prevailed throughout the whole of the Mixteca.

The Mixtecs also established a number of new settlements in the region currently occupied by the city of Oaxaca; the new sites were run by chiefs elected by the lord of Cuilapan. This group extended its dominion as far as the Etla Valley, perhaps even subjugating the people of Huijazóo.

Accounts are confused over how the Mixtec came to overrun places like Mitla and Teitipac in the Tlacolula Valley. Some documents state that the Mixtecs spread through these areas, others that they merely exacted tributes; in either case, some form of political domination was established. The information we have is difficult to analyze properly, because in these years the influence and relations with the Aztecs generated widespread struggles to subdue other peoples by imposing tributes, a characteristic of Aztec policy toward other Mesoamerican peoples. The resulting strife and dissent engendered allegiances among peoples originating in Oaxaca itself, but also with groups from faraway lands, such as the Aztecs, with their ambitions for conquest and domination.

The Archaeological Evidence

Mixtec influence on the Central Valleys is convincingly borne out by the contents of Tomb 7 at Monte Albán. The tomb, with its Zapotec architecture and situation in the Zapotec capital, took archaeologists by surprise when the objects it contained proved to be high-quality artifacts of pure Mixtec manufacture.

The research carried out in Zaachila was useful in dating the contents of Tomb 7 at Monte Albán to the end of the fourteenth century or to the fifteenth century. The central part of the settlement is composed of a complex of bases—built in adobe and earth because stone was hard to come by. South of the main mound a palatial structure was erected similar to those found in other Zapotec sites—rectangular rooms built around a central courtyard. Apparently, after the Zapotec lord from Zaachila had been ousted by the Mixtecs, the new Mixtec leaders constructed or adapted the tombs known as Tomb 1 and Tomb 2.

These tombs, discovered in 1962, are further confirmation of Mixtec presence in the area. The grave goods are not only typically Mixtec in their style and manufacture, but some objects, such as the rings, are almost identical to those discovered in Tomb 7 at Monte Albán, and were without doubt crafted by the same artist. Likewise the form and multicolored decoration of the vessels are obviously the work of Mixtec craftspersons.

The stepped fret motif on the typical Zapotec *tablero* decorating the façade of the tomb and the stucco bas-reliefs on the walls of the antechamber and chamber of Tomb 1 represent figures identified in the Mixtec codices, such as 9 Flower and 5 Flower. The latter is named in the *Codex Nuttall* as the great-grandfather of 6 Water Colored Strips from Yanhuitlán. 6 Water had given his daughter in marriage to 8

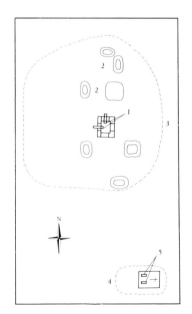

160. Map of Zaachila.
1) Tombs 1 and 2.
2) Unexcavated mounds.
3) Boundary of the main settlement.
4) Boundary of the settlement in San Sebastian.
5) Catholic chapel with Tombs 3 and 4.

194

161. Stucco bas-relief depicting Death on the walls of the mortuary chamber of Tomb 1 at Zaachila.

Deer Fire Serpent. Once again, the presence of people who speak Mixtec in the Miahuatlán Valley, south of Zaachila, tends to imply Mixtec expansion in that direction at the time of the Spanish Conquest.

The tomb explored at Huitzo in the Etla Valley also betrays distinct traces of Mixtec workmanship, particularly in the doorjambs decorating the chamber, which are close in style to those found at Tilantongo in the Mixteca Alta. The same goes for the fine, multicolored craft goods discovered together with the remains of the bones of several individuals. Although the contents are acknowledged as Mixtec, the tomb itself bears many Zapotec features. For a while, Huitzo was a Zapotec center, before being overtaken in the Postclassic Period by the Mixtec.[41] Mitla and Yagul in the Tlacolula Valley also show signs of Mixtec influence in the decoration of certain sites and in various objects, fashioned in Mixtec style.

During the Postclassic Period the various power groups were locked in constant struggle for supremacy, intent on establishing increasingly stable and lasting political entities to insure themselves permanence. Links between high-ranking groups—not only from neighboring political centers, but also between distant ones—became increasingly extensive. Relations became necessarily more complex both within the communities and with the outside world.

Disunity among the various Mixtec communities in a given area sometimes escalated to armed conflict. But friction was more severe with the Aztecs, with their firm rule and tributes. Antagonism was also rife between the inhabitants of the Mixteca Alta and those of Tututepec. All this hostility fanned the flames of expansionism and led to a rise in militarism. Other communities, such as Yanhuitán, at one time governed from twenty-five to thirty different populations, even though the predominant feature was instability and a highly precarious balance of power.

162. Lords 9 Flower (top) and 5 Flower (bottom). Stucco bas-relief on the walls of the mortuary chamber of Tomb 1 at Zaachila (from Whitecotton, 1984).

163. Multicolored terra cotta vessel in the form of a human skull painted white. From Zaachila. Monte Albán V. MNA.

Perhaps one of the most significant characteristics of early Mixtec culture is the jumble of pottery styles, building systems, and urban models, which poses serious problems for archaeologists, whose calculations are based on an analysis of types and models. These obstacles could be overcome by analyzing the bones to establish distinguishing physical characteristics between the Mixtecs and the Zapotecs; this would answer many questions about the sort of influence each group exerted. Was this influence merely cultural? Did it involve imitation of artistic styles and the trade of products? Or was there a real physical presence of the Mixtec group in the Valley of Oaxaca? If so, from what date and at what sites? With such answers we could define a true Mixtec pottery style, distinct from that of Cholula and the Poblana region.

Significant advances in recent years in deciphering the Mixtec codices has greatly facilitated our understanding of this culture. New important details are coming to light in the comparative analysis under way at Tilantongo in the Mixteca Alta, where excavations are being made to verify or locate things described in the codices.

As pointed out above, most of the information currently available to researchers on the pre-Hispanic Mixtecs dates from the Postclassic Period; perspectives on earlier periods have been inferred from these facts. This reasoning, seldom discussed, has caused the Mixtec culture to be mistakenly considered one of the later Mesoamerican cultures. A lot more research must still be done in the earlier sites of Mixteca before a clear overview of this culture can be known.

It is nonetheless a fact that the Mixtecs knew how to adapt to their habitat. First through trade and then through military force, they obtained the necessary means to secure their rule over a vast region. Their overlords, with their elaborate and delicate ornaments, received respect and reverence without equal among the other peoples of the period. With their sovereign craftsmanship in different materials—particularly gold and turquoise—the Mixtecs were among the first artists in the whole of Mesoamerica. At the close of the pre-Hispanic era, once they fell under the yoke of Aztec rule, the Mixtecs were obliged to pay tribute, largely in the form of luxury objects offered to various gods and deposited at the foot of their temples or altars, as borne out by excavations at the Templo Mayor at Tenochtitlán.

Chapter Four
Other Regions of Oaxaca

Chapter Four

Other Regions of Oaxaca

The Cañada

The region of Cañada occupies a strategic position between the valleys of Tehuacán and Oaxaca, offering an important communication route and a highly advantageous habitat in which numerous human groups came to settle. From the time of the first occupation to the arrival of the Spanish, these groups left traces of their passing in their architecture, water-carrying systems, tools, and material objects, and in their scattered bone remains.

The Cañada enjoys a warm climate, and is formed by two rivers, the Río Salado, south of Tehuacán, and the Rió Grande in the north, flowing from the mountains bordering the Valley of Oaxaca. Both rivers join to form the Rió Papaloapan, which empties into the Gulf of Mexico. The valley floor of the Cañada, with a mean height of 2,000 feet (600 meters) above sea level, lies in a deep canyon that provides a cool, temperate climate.

The settlements are distributed along the broad banks of alluvium formed by the Río Grande and its tributaries, where the canyon opens onto a relatively wide valley. For the rest, the terrain is harsh and unsuited for irrigation and therefore uninhabitable.[1] Rainfall in the region is insufficient for good harvest, but some farming is possible on the alluvium along the Río Grande, which can be irrigated with water from the tributaries. This land gives a particularly high yield of around 5 tons of maize per acre (2,000 kilograms per hectare). The lack of frosts in the area makes multiple crop growing also possible. Produce from this area today includes tropical fruits that do not grow in the higher reaches of the Valley of Oaxaca.

Large pre-Hispanic towns like Ouiotepec, Cuicatlán, El Chilar, La Coyotera, and Dominguillo thrived in the rich alluvial soil of the valley floor. The hillsides also hosted important sites, such as Santa Cruz Almoloya, Tecomavaca, Concepción Pápalo, and Santo Domingo, all in vantage points protected from invasion or attacks from hostile outside groups. Nevertheless, their welfare depended on farming the valley floor.

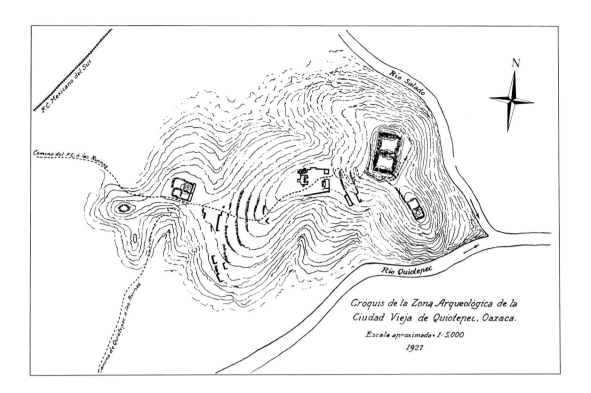

Cróquis de la Zona Arqueológica de la
Ciudad Vieja de Quiotepec, Oaxaca.
Escala aproximada· 1· 5,000
1927

QUIOTEPEC

The most important site by far in the Cañada is Quiotepec, spread out over a series of high terraces overlooking the valley at the confluence of the Río Salado and the Río Grande. To make the most of the site, the occupants filled the gap between two promontories and built high, long containment walls with horizontal rows of hewn stones held together with a mortar of mud. Most of the population lived on the terraces in complex living centers, protected on the west side by a siege wall; the ceremonial area was built on a neighboring peak.

The remains of two large civic, ceremonial complexes include a ball court 246 feet (75 meters) long. As with the buildings, the tombs also evince construction methods similar to those used in the Valley of Oaxaca. The traces of occupation in Quiotepec start from Monte Albán IA; toward the end of Monte Albán II the site had at least five inhabited areas covering no less than 100 acres (40 hectares). Although the city became the capital of the Cañada during Monte Albán III, the presence of fortifications suggests that its ascendancy was not unchallenged by the area's towns. Some scholars consider Quiotepec to be the northernmost center of the Central Valleys under some form of Zapotec control.[2]

CAVERNS FOR RITUAL PURPOSES

Recent discoveries in the area of caverns with paintings, burials, offerings, and other important archaeological and ethnographic material have provided vital clues on the role of the Cuicatecs in the expansion and influence of the Zapotecs and Mixtecs in the Cañada. The use of caverns for ritual purposes goes back to very remote times, and continues to this day; few cult practices have continued uninterrupted for such a length of time. Oaxaca offers a unique opportunity for studying the evolution of these ancestral ceremonies, especially in the region of the Cañada and the Sierra Mazateca. Various archaeological relics bear witness to such ceremonies and to the complexity of ritual in pre-Hispanic times. The accounts of the chroniclers show that these practices continued during the colonial era, and continued to change.

Visitors to the area may see this for themselves in the customs of today's inhabitants of Oaxaca: even today, the inhabitants of the Cañada continue to revere the caverns, and are loath to venture beyond the threshold of the naturally lit parts of the cave. In pre-Hispanic times the common people had a deep fear of encountering some supernatural entity, but there were always those who, overcoming their initial apprehension, pushed ever deeper into the darkness, sometimes risking their lives. Unseen by others, the priests celebrated obscure rites in the depths of the caverns, and were vested with special powers. A common dread of the unknown, of what went on in that awful darkness, induced the community to blindly trust the priests.

According to Marcelo Carmagnani, the indigenous concept of space was hierarchical. For these people there were close links between divine hierarchy and spatial hierarchy. The heavens and the underworld, i.e., the underground, were the exclusive domain of the gods; earthly space was allotted to humankind. This distinction spurred humans to seek contact with their gods in those exclusive, uninhabitable places, which they saw as being closer to the gods themselves—the deep caverns and hilltops, sacred spots that became ceremonial sites.[3]

The caverns explored in the region of the Cañada fall into two categories: those used as living spaces, and those for ceremonial purposes. The cave explored by Moser in 1966–67, the Cueva de Ejutla, belongs to this second category and consists of forty-five cells, certainly used for depositing bodies, possibly in the Postclassic Period. The cave yielded remains of torches, colored plumage, agave thorns, obsidian knives, and fine cords for the ceremonies of ritual bloodletting.[4]

In the nearby Mazatec region the exploration of the Cueva de Tenango brought to light various burials associated with multicolored vessels and other finely worked material corresponding to the Postclassic Period.[5]

In 1985 another cavern, the Cueva de la Navaja, was found to consist of three chambers containing skeletal remains of several individuals, together with rich funeral offerings. The inventory includes sixty vessels, and various stone artifacts, beads, and figures in greenstone, obsidian knives, and other objects made in shell, jade, coral, fish bone, or from the bones of dogs. The materials, all datable to the Preclassic and Postclassic periods, were grouped into offerings; the most numerous group includes forty-four pieces of pottery.[6]

A natural cavern called the Abrigo Escondido, presents interesting traces of pre-Hispanic occupation. The entrance faces the Río de las Vueltas in the southern Cañada, near the archaeological site of La Coyotera. The cavern is 121 feet (37 meters) wide and 56 feet (17 meters) deep, with a maximum height of 33 feet (10 meters). The walls are extensively decorated with paintings depicting rituals, some featuring iguanas, serpents, deer, and other animals, while others feature humans or geometric patterns. There are also many handprints in both negative and positive painting techniques. Toward the mouth of the cavern there are many fragments of palm matting and other vegetable fiber, clearly used for covering the bodies of those buried there. The cavern is nonetheless unexplored and is due to be fully investigated shortly.

CUEVA DE LA ESTRELLA

This last example involves the discovery of important material made last year by a group of North American speleologists, or cave explorers, in Cueva de la Estrella, where research has been under way since 1986. In early 1990 the anthropologist Lourdes Márquez, the archaeologist Marcus Winter, and I carried out surveying and some archaeological fieldwork in the cavern, assisted by Janet Fitzsimmons, Bill Steele, Bill Stone, and other speleologists.

Situated cast of Cuicatlán at about 9,800 feet (3,000 meters) above sea level and 7,550 feet (2,300 meters) above the Río Grande, this cavern has a main entrance 98 feet (30 meters) wide and 20 feet (6 meters) high, leading to a spacious chamber 230 feet (70 meters) wide, 656 feet (200 meters) long, and 98 feet (30 meters) high. The chamber leads to three long tunnels, two running toward the south and one extending toward the west for several hundred yards. The main chamber slopes down thirty degrees toward the back. In the center stands a rectangular platform, 33 feet (10 meters) long and 13 feet (4 meters) wide, jutting out of the natural slope of the cave floor.

Scattered on and around the platform at some distance we found the remains of various individuals wrapped in palm matting and deposited on a layer of *zacate,* or grass, and covered in a layer of the same. Some of these burials had disintegrated, others were well-preserved. Besides the bone remains we found an assortment of vessels—some intact—dating from the Classic and Postclassic periods. Other finds include small obsidian knives, a spearhead, and a series of small spheres of green, white, and gray stone. A wooden mask was also found, in pieces, decorated with mosaic in turquoise, very similar to the one discovered in the Cueva de Ejutla.

Continuing the exploration in one of the tunnels running south, the speleologists had to lower themselves by rope down a vertical shaft to another tunnel 130 feet (40 meters) below; here they came across a hollow containing an offering composed of ceramic and alabaster vessels, and a small, red-painted statue of a god, rather crudely fashioned from small stones and mud. Today the cavern is frequented by novitiates and seers, who enter the main chamber through a secondary tunnel, carry out their rites, and leave the cave floor strewn with bones of birds, eggs, plant remains, coins, lists of names, and personal objects. They never stray into the tunnel containing the archaeological remains, however, partly in deference and veneration, and partly for fear of their ancient gods.

Besides the material listed above, the cavern also produced two wooden plaques covered in turquoise mosaic depicting signs executed in the style of the codices. Both plaques were split in half, one face-down on the bare ground; it had lost much of its original mosaic. The other was face-up and had at least half left. Together with these plaques, which were found in alcoves formed from large stones, was a vessel containing ten scraps of greenstone. One of the plaques is designed with a central sun motif surrounded by no less than fifteen different figures, warriors, and slaves; some wear bird-shaped helmets, others are guarding a kneeling prisoner with a wooden collar about his neck. There is also a temple and a ball court. The other

165. Wooden board with turquoise mosaic executed in codex style. From Cueva de la Estrella in the Cañada region. Monte Albán III. MRO.

202

plaque depicts a solar disk or shield pierced by three arrows. The piece is beautiful-ly worked with an infinite number of tiny fragments of turquoise; the artist has used the different tones of the precious stone to trace out the various figures and main elements in light blue against a background of dark blue. The frame around the wooden plaque is also completely covered in turquoise mosaic.

In addition to this extraordinary design and the artist's skill, it is interesting to note that the turquoise is worked with the same technique used for a set of fragments found in Tomb 1 at Zaachila, i.e., minute figures of tiny, light-colored *tesserae* against a darker background.

In the preceding chapter we commented on Mixtec expansion in the Central Valleys of Oaxaca; today, with the discovery of this material we must seriously consider the possibility of a permanent Mixtec occupation of this region of the Cañada, or perhaps only a temporary submission, and the use of the caverns for burying the prominent members of the community. Linguistic studies indicate how the Mixtec and Cuicatec language split off from the same Otomanguean root. A careful study of the fragments found in this cavern will perhaps shed light on some of the numerous doubts surrounding the development of this region in pre-Hispanic times.

The Coast

From the archaeological point of view, the coastal area is still relatively uncharted. Research along the Pacific shoreline for the 190 miles (300 kilometers) stretching from the Isthmus of Tehuantepec to the basin of the Río Verde in the west has offered few clues on human occupation in the area. The terrain is largely composed of intrusive, untempered igneous rock, which has generated a very sandy soil. The few valleys along the bays contain alluvial and coastal deposits, making them rather unsuitable for agriculture. The Río Verde valley, however, offers highly advantageous conditions for farming, and in fact numerous signs of human settlement from the Preclassic Period have been found in the area. A spacious plain networked by a lagoon-estuary offered the valley inhabitants a mixed diet of crops and seafood, which was particularly abundant along the coastal waters. Comparative studies are currently being made on bone remains found in this area and in the Central Valleys of Oaxaca in order to get a more accurate picture of their diet.[7]

In pre-Hispanic times trade along the Mesoamerican coast was intense, as proved by the exchange of manufactured items and raw materials between regions at some considerable distance from each other. This was how the first skills in working gold and silver reach Oaxaca from Central and South America. The results of comparative studies into social organizations, architectural styles, and pottery types are not as definitive as one would hope, owing to the mixing and permeability among what are considered to be the distinguishing features of each social group. But this mosaic of cultural elements is characteristic of the groups inhabiting the coast.

Evidence of human occupation in the coastal region dates back to 500 B.C.E., more or less contemporary with the foundation of Monte Albán in the Central Valleys. Some authors also mention the presence of Chontal groups, who penetrated through the Isthmus of Tehuantepec.[8]

In the Classic Period the sites of Nopala and Río Grande were occupied by groups of Chatinos belonging to the Otomanguean linguistic group. Nopala lies some 19 miles (30 kilometers) north of today's Puerto Escondido, and is situated partly on human-built terracing on the slopes of a hill known as Cerro de la Igle-

166. Stela with bas-relief of an important figure with his arms crossed, and a large headdress in the form of a jaguar. The lower section features calendrical glyphs. From Río Grande, in the Mixteca de la Costa region. Monte Albán V. MNA.

169. Partial map of Guiengola.
1) Central plaza.
2) East Temple.
3) West Temple.
4) Ball Court.
5) Palacio.
6) Wall.
7) Río Tehuantepec.

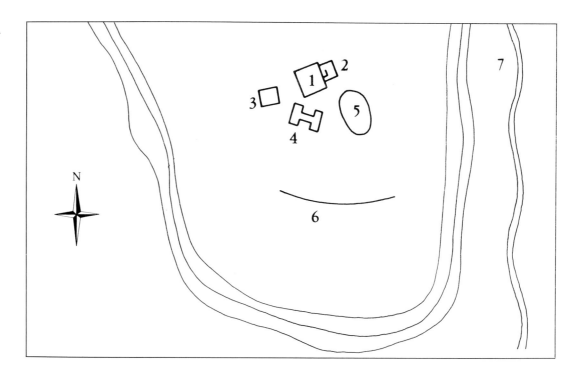

shaped tombs in the Central Valleys of Oaxaca, though here there are additional chambers at the ends of the wings; regrettably, both tombs were sacked and nothing is known of their original contents.[12]

The Aztecs used the Isthmus region as an important corridor for their incoming tribute from the affluent region of Soconusco. According to Francisco de Burgoa, some Aztec merchants were attacked and slain by the Zapotecs at Tehuantepec toward the end of the fifteenth century. The Aztec king Ahuízotl sent his troops in counterattack, but his attempts to take the Zapotec governor Cocijoeza prisoner failed because Cocijoeza had Tehuantepec fortified and, after arming the town of Guiengola, held back the Aztec incursion for nearly seven months. The Aztecs had to split their forces in two to attack the two towns at the same time. The mountain on which Guiengola was built was too large to besiege, and so the assailants were forced to make a frontal attack on the most heavily fortified front, which was made even more inaccessible by the dense hillside vegetation. Apparently, the Zapotecs waged guerrilla warfare, making rapid night raids on the scattered groups of Aztec soldiers, whom they killed and carried back to the camp. Later, to heal relations, the two groups arranged a marriage between Cocijoeza and Ichcatlaxoch, the daughter of the *tlatoani* (the Aztec governor) known by the name of Pelaxilla. The union brought forth a son, Cocijopii, who succeeded his father, but relations between his people and the Aztecs, then led by Motecuhzoma II, were never entirely harmonious. When the Spanish made their way into the Isthmus, the Zapotec governor befriended them—to rid himself of the Aztec peril—little knowing what was to transpire.

Appendix
The Zapotec Tomb at Huijazóo
by María Luisa Franco Brizuela

Appendix

The Zapotec Tomb at Huijazóo

by María Luisa Franco Brizuela

The pre-Hispanic tomb discussed here is situated 18 miles (29 kilometers) northwest of today's town of Oaxaca in the municipality of Suchilquitongo, in the Etla Valley. The tomb is part of a ceremonial center which, though not yet excavated, can be clearly made out and lies on a hill 1.2 miles (2 kilometers) long and 300 feet (90 meters) high.

The *Relaciones Geográficas de Oaxaca,*[1] written by Bartolomé de Zárate in the sixteenth century, includes the *Relación Geográfica de Guaxilotitlan* (today San Pablo Huitzo), dated March 10, 1581. The report speaks of a village called Xochiquitongo (today Santiago Suchilquitongo) as one of the settlements subject to that place.

The tomb at Huijazóo was catalogued Tomb 5 by its discoverer, the archaeologist Enrique Méndez of the Instituto Nacional de Antropología e Historia. The tomb was discovered in November 1985, and was first entered on November 23. Registered as Tomb 5 of Platform 1 beneath Mound G, the tomb has been attributed to the Zapotec culture, and dated to the last third of the Classic Period, between 650 and 900 C.E. In a later period the tomb was reoccupied by the Mixtecs.

From the platform over the tomb one can see the Etla Valley in the distance, the town of Oaxaca, Monte Albán, the Sierra Madre of Oaxaca, and the Sierra Madre of the South. Closer by lie the village of Santiago Suchilquitongo, some red stone quarries, and the main road linking Oaxaca with Mexico City, running close to the archaeological site.

The tomb lies along a north–south axis, with the entrance in the southern side, and is constructed below a platform covered by a small mound created by centuries of deposits of Mixtec paving, earth, and stones. The tomb lies at a depth of 11.8 feet (3.6 meters) and is accessed by a short stairway, cut out from a kind of "cube of light," consisting of nine well-preserved steps in stone and stuccoed earth.

The tomb is composed of three parts—Antechamber I, small and with two narrow niches; Antechamber II, wide and with a sunken floor creating a kind of courtyard, two large side niches, and four smaller corner niches called *esquineros*; and the Mortuary Chamber.

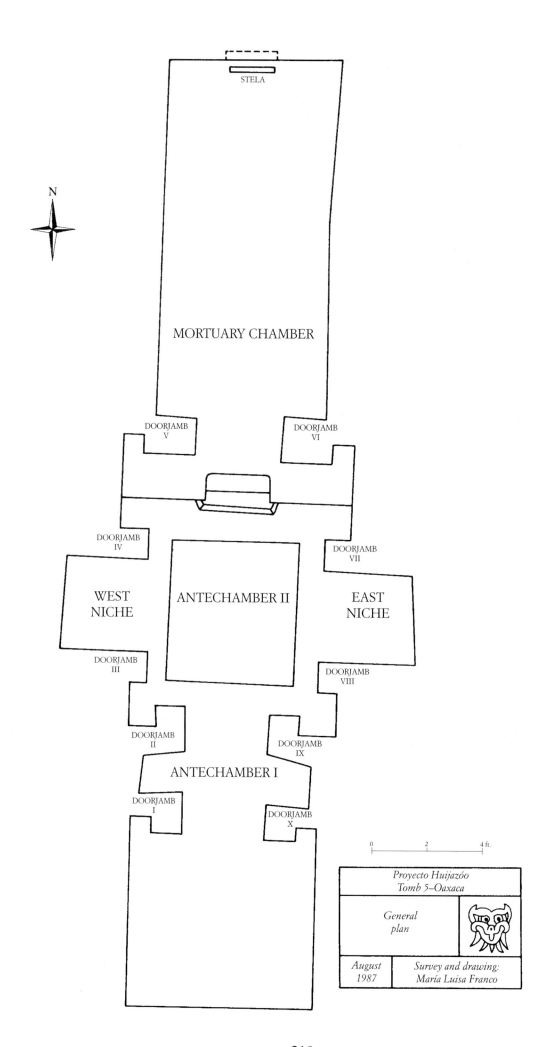

MORTUARY CHAMBER

STELA

DOORJAMB
V

DOORJAMB
VI

DOORJAMB
IV

DOORJAMB
VII

WEST
NICHE

ANTECHAMBER II

EAST
NICHE

DOORJAMB
III

DOORJAMB
VIII

DOORJAMB
II

DOORJAMB
IX

ANTECHAMBER I

DOORJAMB
I

DOORJAMB
X

N

0   2   4 ft.

Proyecto Huijazóo
Tomb 5–Oaxaca

General
plan

August
1987

Survey and drawing:
María Luisa Franco

170. Plan of Tomb 5 at
Huijazóo.

The complex is lined with ten doorjambs, which serve as pillars for five lintels and are decorated with bas-reliefs covered in red pigment. Each doorjamb measures 4.6 feet (1.4 meters) high and 13.8 inches (35 centimeters) wide, except for the double jambs, which are 23.6 inches (60 centimeters) wide. The doorjambs and lintels are each made from a single block of stone.

The walls are formed with squared-off slabs of pink stone. The roofing consists of large slabs of pink stone, all set at an angle except for those in Antechamber I, which has a flat roof of small rectangular stones. The flooring consists of compacted, smooth mortar mixed with stone and faced in stucco.

The full length of the tomb is 28.9 feet (8.81 meters), and its maximum width is 13.3 feet (4.05 meters); the Mortuary Chamber is 8 feet (2.45 meters) high, and Antechamber II is 12.1 feet (3.7 meters) high.

The images depicted on the walls of the tomb range from geometric designs to human figures, with glyphs, plant motifs, and animal-shaped figures. Though some figures resemble each other closely, there are various slight distinguishing features and colors.

The painting shows the influence of the Teotihuacán and Maya styles. There are also various highly curious technical features, such as the heavy brushstrokes and dribbles of color on the walls, or the rapid strokes that merely suggest the figures; in various points one can detect where alterations were made, without canceling the original. The stonework is embellished with particularly fine engravings, and the walls finished and smoothed down with great care.

Any iconographic description must be done with the utmost accuracy in capturing each individual detail in its proper context to enable scholars to make their interpretations: each line, color, item of clothing, and attribute is part of the rich language of every pre-Hispanic culture, and deserves a thorough and careful interpretation.

The Façade

The entrance to the tomb is surmounted by a lintel covered in stucco, with a red circle and a horizontal red bar painted on it. The lintel supports a *tablero a doble escapulario*, resting on a low *talud*.

The center of the *tablero*, of which only the ends are visible, is occupied by a large high-relief serpent-jaguar head with its jaws open, exposing its teeth, fangs, corrugated palate, and forked tongue; emerging from its jaws is the head of a bird with curved beak and pronounced round eyes. The serpent's eyes are represented frontally at either side of the open jaws. An uneven stripe of red pigment runs from the serpent's nostrils to the tip of its tongue; the same red color is used for the upper gums. On either side of the jaws are various motifs in relief—volutes (spiral or scroll-shaped forms) and straight lines, echoed by similar motifs on the *talud*, just below the jaw of the serpent. Over the head are two square forms and an inverted central triangle.

The entire representation is carved into the stone and coated in stucco.

Antechamber I

The walls of the two narrow side niches are a reddish-orange color, and decorated with a great many figures, regrettably very faded. The back wall of the east niche bears two faces in profile painted in ocher, brown, and green with black outlines,

171. Entrance to Tomb 5 at Huijazóo.

172. Detail of the *tablero* on the façade of Tomb 5 at Huijazóo, decorated with a large serpent-jaguar head with the head of a bird emerging from its jaws.

and two other indistinct motifs in the same colors. On the back wall of the west niche one can make out a bird's head in profile in ocher. Further down, there are four horizontal bands bordered in black; the two on the left are rectangular, while those on the right look like twisted cords. Scattered traces of green and brown paint are visible, and in the right-hand corner is a large area of dark red.

The lintels have also been colored. On the north face of Lintel 1 there are some pink glyphs with black outline. There is no stucco here, and the pigment is applied

173. Mural on the north face of Lintel 1, in Antechamber I of Tomb 5 at Huijazóo. A human profile can be seen on the left.

directly to the stone. Among the various symbols and geometric patterns there is a human profile and, perhaps, the head of a monkey. The south face of Lintel 2 is more heavily decorated, with glyphs, red, black, and white patterns, all outlined in black, making use of the white surface as a background. Among the many symbols is a profile above a hand, a serpent, and some numerals.

The glyphs may refer to the place, dates, and person buried in the tomb.

Antechamber II

The second antechamber has a sunken central section, and three steps up to the mortuary chamber proper. The doorjambs at the entrance to the chamber include a small *tablero a doble escapulario*, each resting on a low *talud*, replicating the three large *tableros* surmounting the side niches and the entrance of the antechamber. Both jambs and lintels are stuccoed, and the lintels are decorated with a simple red square at the center (see color plates 86 and 89).

THE MASK

Unlike the others, the *tablero* over the entrance to the mortuary chamber has a large stucco mask in high-relief, depicting a large jaguar head with open jaws; the corners of the upper lip are curved downward, exposing the fangs and the jaw on which the jutting tongue rests. The jaguar's ears are small, and it is wearing a head-dress with various geometric patterns culminating in the year symbol. On either side of the head are two stripe-shapes with circles and other motifs, including a bat's wings.

From the jaguar's jaws emerges a figure with a bat's head and human arms; the face is given an intense gaze by outlining the irises and pupils of the eyes in black; the nostrils are painted red. The slightly parted lips reveal fangs and a small tongue; two circular earrings adorn the tiny pointed ears. The arms jut outward and hands are resting on two small protrusions (see color plate 89).

213

All the walls of Antechamber II, including those bearing the four *esquineros*, are painted in reddish-orange, but the two large niches also have various figurative elements.

The back wall (east) of the East Niche (see color plate 92) is decorated with four personages in profile, two on either side, facing each other. Apart from some minor details, their clothing, headdresses, personal ornaments, and facial features are identical. They are wearing a short cape of *quezquémitl*, with a pointed flap down the back, decorated with horizontal stripes of ocher, brown, and white of different widths, and a short skirt with the same pattern; the sandals are merely suggested by a white thong around the ankle, tied at the front. The black hair is gathered on the top of the head with a white ribbon, with a fringe at the front. All the figures have ocher-colored faces with elongated eyes, short curved noses, and pronounced lips and receding chin. All sport white ear plugs. Some scholars believe these figures to represent cloth-weavers, given the circular black and white instruments in their hands.

THE WEST NICHE

The back wall (west) of this niche (see color plate 87) is decorated with two personages in profile, sitting face-to-face, with tall, elaborate headdresses in which one can make out the heads of birds with rich plumage. The figures are naked except for a breechcloth. Between them stands a kind of basket containing three unidentifiable objects. The background is colored reddish-orange, darker in some places, the figures outlined in black, and the ornaments and headgear painted in ocher, white, green, and red.

The two side walls of the West Niche are painted with various figures arranged in two bands: the figures in the upper band—some of which are very large—are all clothed in sumptuous attire, whereas the figures in the lower band are warriors of varying status, judging from the relative simplicity or elaborateness of their attire and weapons.

On the right-hand wall north of the niche the two bands are divided by a white stripe.

The upper band shows two large figures in profile with dark red skin: the one on the right, a female figure, is by far the more imposing and more finely drawn (see color plate 97). Her features are typically Maya—elongated eyes, short nose, pronounced lips, smooth black hair; there is a clearly visible hump on her back. Her clothing is luxurious and comprises a bird with rich ocher and green plumage, ear plugs, large eyes, forked tongue, and fangs, and from whose beak a striking motif flows out over the face of the woman; from her headdress emerges a long, decorated band reaching almost to the ground. The figure probably represents a priestess. Her ornaments include circular ocher and green ear plugs, and a necklace of mixed round and square green and white beads. She is wearing a dark red *quezquémitl* bordered in white with black stripes, a belt (also white with black stripes) of which the two ends are visible, and a green pleated dress with horizontal stripes of ocher and red, reaching to her ankles. She is barefoot. In her right hand is a bag for *copal* (a typical attribute of priestesses), and in her left she carries an object perhaps linked to fertility. From her mouth issues the scroll sign indicating speech, with two simple whorls. The entire image is outlined in black on a reddish-orange background, with strong colors: green, red, ocher, and white. Level with the arm there are signs of an alteration consisting of two horizontal black lines that were not completely obliterated.

The lower band on this wall shows three figures (see color plate 96), presumably of inferior status given their simpler attire of white breechcloths, green-and-white necklaces, green ear plugs, and a headdress (the same for each) of green plumes with elements in ocher and brown. Each figure holds an ornate spear in one hand; the other is raised to mouth-height. Their bodies are difficult to make out due to the deterioration of the stucco.

The left side wall south of the niche also shows two bands separated by a white stripe.

The upper band shows three lavishly attired figures, one of whom, in addition to a superb headdress, ear plugs, and necklace of large green beads, carries an elaborate spear, a bag for *copal*, and a kind of shield depicting a bat's head, attached to his belt.

The lower band presents five figures, each dressed in something resembling a cape of white feathers reaching down to the ankles. Their headdresses are made of green and ocher feathers, and their spears are of varying design.

The Mortuary Chamber

The figurative elements still visible today in this imposing room are all on the side walls (east and west) and on an engraved stela at the back. Most of the original decorations on the north wall have disappeared, but one can still make out a headdress of green feathers with profiles of ocher-eyed birds with ocher and red beaks peeping out.

THE EAST WALL

This wall presents two bands separated with a white stripe, decorated with a row of figures in black outline against an orange background (see color plate 93).

The upper band offers a row of nine figures facing the back wall. The faces are corroded and therefore indistinct, but the green feathered costumes are still vivid. The figures are all dressed alike: a smock with decorations in white, brown, and ocher; a green breastplate decorated with a small face; green circular ear plugs; and sandals. Their headgear, however, varies. The first two on the left are wearing green plumage, long brown supports hanging down behind to the ground, and a bird's head from whose beak hang three green teardrop shapes. The headdress worn by the other seven consists of a wide base of many twined black lines surmounted by green plumage, and a kind of white belt worn down the back. The objects in their hands resemble rattles.

The lower band also shows nine figures (see color plate 98) but quite different from those above. The first three from the left also wear belts, green necklaces, and cup-shaped headdresses with green and ocher stripes. They are carrying spears and *copal* bags. The other six figures are magnificently garbed in the same kind of knee-length costume decorated with various geometric patterns in brown, white, and green. Their faces are covered by a kind of helmet with a visor similar to those worn by the ball players of Dainzú. In one hand they clutch a bunch of three green strips resembling a lily, and in the other a brown, semicircular object (perhaps a ball, or a device for throwing one). Ignacio Bernal describes them thus:

215

Not one of the players has his head exposed. Instead it is encased inside a sort of wooden head-piece, closed at the back, with a visor over the face similar to those worn in fencing. ... Without exception, they carry a ball in their right hand.[2]

Each figure sports a highly elaborate headdress, each one different except for the long geometric bands down the back in green, black, and white; the front is decorated with the likeness of a god and his relative attributes: a jaguar, a serpent, the long-nosed god, the skinless god, a human skull, a bird, and so on.

THE WEST WALL

The west wall (see color plate 90) also presents two horizontal bands of figures, one above the other. The background color is uniformly orange, and once again the figures are outlined in black.

The upper band pictures a row of ten, more or less identical, elderly figures with dark skin and wrinkled cheeks, toothless mouths, and beards pointing outward. Their expressions are jubilant, however. Each headdress is composed of a large, full-length bird with semihuman features, perched on a green base, a rich crown of feathers, a long beak, and tail. The figures are also dressed alike, with green ear plugs; necklaces of white (or green) beads extending down the backs almost to the ground; smocks with a wavy ocher and green pattern; strange, semi-curved belts; and no shoes. In front of each one is the scrolling speech sign. They hold instruments decorated in black and ocher.

The lower band shows nine more figures, identical to those in the lower band on the East Wall, arranged in the same order, except that here five figures have black arms and legs.

The Doorjambs

As we have seen, the tomb has ten doorjambs made of a single slab of stone, engraved with bas-reliefs and painted in a striking red applied directly onto the surface of the stone.

Each jamb features a standing figure in profile (see color plate 91). Whether representing a man or a jaguar-man, each figure is strikingly dressed in a smock, ear plugs, *copal* bag, staff, sandals, richly plumed bird headdress, weapons, and shield. The upper part of each jamb is inscribed with glyphs, numerals, and the "Jaws of Heaven" symbol found in the Zapotec tombs, such as Tomb 5 at Monte Albán.

The two jambs on either side of the entrance to the Mortuary Chamber (Doorjambs V and VI) are of double thickness and bear two figures: a jaguar-man, and a barefoot priestess wearing a *huipil*, an ankle-length skirt, ear plugs, and a necklace.

The Stela

The stela in the mortuary chamber is relatively small and is carved in bas-relief on the front and sides. The entire stela is painted a vibrant red.

Two scenes are represented in bas-relief, one above the other, divided by a horizontal band. Along the top half are a series of glyphs and numerals. Below these is a young man, shown in profile, with finely carved features, sitting barefoot on a woven base on the left. He is naked to the waist, and wears a shirt; his personal ornaments include a necklace, ear plugs, and a cone-shaped headdress with plumage and vari-

Opposite:

86. Antechamber II. South side with access to Antechamber I and, on right, access to the West Niche. Note the tableros a doble escapulario *and low* talud, *the lintels with squares of red paint in the center, the nomolithic doorjambs decorated with bas-reliefs painted red, and the sunken floor forming a sort of small internal patio.*

87. Top: *Antechamber II. The West Niche with doorjambs decorated with bas-reliefs and murals.*

88. Bottom: *Antechamber II. The East Niche, also decorated with bas-reliefs and murals.*

Opposite:

89. *Antechamber II. North side, with access to the Mortuary Chamber. Noticeable from the top are the* tablero a doble escapulario *decorated with a high-relief stucco mask resting on a low* talud, *the lintel with a square of red paint, the twin doorjambs decorated with bas-reliefs, painted red, resting on two small* tableros *with a* talud, *and another two* tableros *at the sides of the steps leading up into the Mortuary Chamber.*

90. Above: *Mortuary Chamber, west wall. The upper band of the mural shows a procession of elderly figures; at the back of the chamber is a stela with bas-relief motifs painted red.*

91. Near right: *Doorjamb in Antechamber II. The bas-relief depicts a priest.*

92. Far right: *Four spinners. Mural on the back wall of the East Niche of Antechamber II.*

Opposite:

93. Top: *Mortuary Chamber, east wall. The upper band has a mural of a row of figures wearing headdresses with green feathers.*

94. 95. Bottom left: *Mortuary Chamber, south wall.* Bottom right: *Mortuary Chamber, north wall. Note the large sloping slabs of the roof.*

Pages 222–23:

96. *Three figures armed with spears. Mural on the lower part of the north wall of the West Niche in Antechamber II.*

97. *Priestess richly dressed with a bag for her* copal. *The mural, one of the finest and best-preserved of Tomb 5, is on the upper band of the north wall of the West Niche in Antechamber II.*

98. Above: *Ball players. Mural on the lower band of the east wall of the Mortuary Chamber.*

ous ornaments. In his outstretched hands he holds a vase with a bird perched on it, together with a toothed instrument, and another unidentified object. Opposite the youth is a mature male figure, evidently of higher rank, with roughly drawn features, seated on a high platform. With one exposed arm the man holds a strange pleated garment, which covers him from head to toe; he is also wearing necklaces, elaborate ear plugs, and a striking headdress depicting the long-nosed god decorated with plumage, ear plugs and a necklace, and one arm bent with the palm of his hand turned upward. The lower scene also shows two figures. On the left sits a woman in a *quezquémitl*, *huipil*, and plaited hair with plumage. On the right sits a bearded old man naked to the waist, with a wizened face and amicable expression. His headdress is similar to the youth's. The two figures sit facing each other on identical woven bases, and each holds a vase with objects indentical to those in the boy's. The upper part of the scene is once again decorated with glyphs and numerals.

Conclusion

To summarize briefly, various figures described above—particularly those in the mortuary chamber—most probably symbolize the underworld. The ball game was sometimes linked to the world of the dead.

In the decapitation scene in the ball court at Chichén Itzá, a ball player is holding a ball or ball thrower in his right hand, an object almost identical to those held by the figures in the mortuary chamber of Tomb 5.

The rest of the figures represent different personalities and roles, and belong to different scenes. They include deities, priests, priestesses, warriors, and other figures whose meaning might soon be unraveled and hence explain the entire set of paintings.

Given the importance of this Zapotec tomb and the abundance of murals it contains, urgent conservation and restoration measures were necessary, as the tomb was damaged and left buried for so many centuries in a high-risk earthquake zone; further damage has occurred through deterioration and natural decay.

In 1987 the Dirección de Restauración del Patrimonio Cultural of the Instituto Nacional de Antropología e Historia approved a conservation project coordinated by the author, which will focus in minute detail on all aspects of the tomb. The project will involve state-of-the-art technology and procedures in full compliance with international standards.

the great conqueror 8 Deer Jaguar Claw. The first marriage was between two children of 8 Deer and probably his fourth wife. The man was called 8 Movement and the woman 8 Grass, both born after 1060 C.E. The second marriage was between two of 8 Deer's great-grandchildren, both firstborn, who lived in the twelfth century: the man was 8 Reed, king of Tilantongo, the woman was his sister and her name was 5 Rabbit. The third and fourth marriages involved the royal dynasties of Tilantongo and Teozacoalco, corresponding with the sixth generation after 8 Deer; the king of Tilantongo, 12 Reed, married his elder sister 3 Jaguar. The king of Teozacoalco, 12 House, married one of his younger sisters, 11 Lizard.

19. Herrera y Tordesillas, 1947, III: 98.
20. Dahlgren, 1954: 170-73.
21. Caso, 1938: 50.
22. Gaxiola, 1984: 75-80.
23. Scholars think that the Nuiñe culture flourished in the Classic Period, between 300 and 800 C.E.
24. Paddock, 1970: 200.
25. Whitecotton, 1984: 89.
26. Burgoa, 1934-35. Caso, 1949. Del Paso y Troncoso, 1905-8.
27. Caso, 1960. Byland and Pohl, 1988.
28. Dahlgren, 1954: 188.
29. Burgoa, 1934-35. García, 1729.
30. Simonin, 1989.
31. García, 1729.
32. Caso, 1969: 92.
33. Burgoa, 1934-35.
34. Caso, 1984.
35. Caso, 1984, I: 16-19.
36. Seler, 1901-2; 1902-3; 1963.
37. Whitecotton, 1984: 90.
38. Barlow, 1945: 23.
39. Whitecotton, 1984: 94.
40. Burgoa, 1934-35, I: 395-96.
41. Whitecotton, 1984: 97.

CHAPTER 4

1. Hunt and Hunt, 1974: 135-37.
2. Redmon and Spencer, 1983: 119.
3. Carmagnani, 1988: 30.
4. Moser, 1975: 25-36.
5. Winter, 1984.
6. Fitzsimmons, n.d.
7. Arthur A. Joyce, personal note (1989).
8. Long, 1974: 95.
9. For more information on this subject, see Caso, 1984.
10. Fernández and Gómez, 1988: 18.
11. Zeitlin and Zeitlin, 1990: 400-36.
12. Peterson, 1990: 460-63.

APPENDIX

1. Del Paso y Troncoso, 1981.
2. Bernal, 1969b.

Bibliography

Abbreviations:
    ADEVA, Akademische Druck- und Verlagsanstalt
    INAH, Instituto Nacional de Antropología e Historia
    SEP, Secretaría de Educación Pública
    SMA, Sociedad Mexicana de Antropología
    UNAM, Universidad Nacional Autónoma de México

ACOSTA, JORGE
n.d.   "Informes de la XIII, XIV, XV, XVI y XVII temporadas de
            exploraciones arqueológicas en Monte Albán, de los
            años 1944 a 1949." Unpublished manuscripts and re-
            ports of the Archivio de la Dirección de Monumentos
            Prehispánicos. Mexico City: INAH.
1965   "Preclassic and Classic Architecture of Oaxaca," *Hand-
            book of Middle American Indians,* vol. 3, Robert Wau-
            chope (ed.): 814-36. Austin: University of Texas Press.
ACUÑA, RENÉ
1984   *Relaciones Geográficas del Siglo XVI: Antequera,* vol. 2.
            Mexico City: UNAM.
ALCINA FRANCH, JOSÉ
1972   "Los dioses del panteón zapoteco," *Anales de
            Antropología,* vol. IX: 9-43. Mexico City: UNAM.
BARLOW, ROBERT H.
1945   "Dos relaciones antiguas del pueblo de Cuilapan, Esta-
            do de Oaxaca," *Tlalocan* (Mexico City) 2: 18-28.
1946   "Relación de Antequera," *Tlalocan* (Mexico City) 2:
            134-37.
BERNAL, IGNACIO
1968   "The Olmec Presence in Oaxaca," *Mexico Quarterly
            Review* 3, I: 6-22.
1969   "El Juego de Pelota más antiguo en México," *Artes de
            México* (Mexico City) no. 119, vol. xv.
1970   "The Mixtecs in the Archaeology of the Valley of Oaxa-
            ca," *Ancient Oaxaca,* John Paddock (ed.): 345-66. Stan-
            ford, California: Stanford University Press.
BERNAL, IGNACIO, and LORENZO GAMIO
1974   *Yagul: el Palacio de los Seis Patios.* Mexico City: Institu-
            to de Investigaciones Antropológicas, UNAM.
BLANTON, RICHARD E.
1978   *Monte Albán: Settlement Patterns at the Ancient Zapotec
            Capital.* New York: Academic Press.
BLANTON, RICHARD E., STEPHEN A. KOWALEWSKI, GARY M. FEINMAN,
and LAURA M. FINSTEN
1993   *Ancient Mesoamerica: A Comparison of Change in Three
            Regions.* Cambridge: 2nd ed. Cambridge University Press.
BLANTON, RICHARD E., STEPHEN A. KOWALEWSKI, GARY M. FEINMAN,
and JILL APPEL
1982   *Monte Albán's Hinterland, Part I: Prehispanic Settlement*

*Patterns of the Central and Southern Parts of the Valley
of Oaxaca, Mexico.* Memoirs of the Museum of Anthropology. N. 15, Ann Arbor: University of Michigan.
BURGOA, FRAY FRANCISCO DE
1989   *Geográfica descripción.* Biblioteca Porrúa N. 97, 2 vols.
            [1674]. Mexico City: Editorial Porrúa.
1989   *Palestra Historial.* Biblioteca Porrúa N. 94, [1670].
            Mexico City: Editorial Porrúa.
BYLAND, BRUCE E., and JOHN M. D. POHL
1994   *In the Realm of 8 Deer. The Archaeology of the Mixtec
            Codices.* Norman, Oklahoma: University of Oklahoma
            Press.
CARMAGNANI, MARCELO
1988   *El regreso de los dioses.* Mexico City: Fondo de Cultura
            Económica.
CASO, ALFONSO
1933   "Las tumbas de Monte Albán, *Anales del Museo Na-
            cional de Arqueología, Historia y Etnología,* series IV,
            vol. 8: 641-48. Mexico City: INAH.
1938   *Exploraciones en Oaxaca, quinta y sexta temporadas
            (1936-1937)* Informe no. 34. Mexico City: Instituto
            Panamericano de Geografía e Historia.
1949   *"El mapa de Teozacoalco," Cuadernos Americanos* (Mex-
            ico City) 8, 5: 145-81.
1954   *Interpretación del Códice Gómez de Orozco.* Mexico
            City.
1960   "Valor histórico de los Códices mixtecos," *Cuadernos
            Americanos* (Mexico City) 19, 2: 139-47.
1961   *Los Lienzos Mixtecos de Ihuitlán y Antonio de León.*
            Mexico City.
1965   "Mixtec Writing and Calendar," *Handbook of Middle
            American Indians,* vol. 3, Robert Wauchope (ed.): 948-
            61. Austin: University of Texas Press.
1969   *El Tesoro de Monte Albán,* Memorias del Instituto Na-
            cional de Antropología e Historia no. III. Mexico City:
            INAH.
1984   *Reyes y Reinos de la Mixteca,* 2 vols. Mexico City: Fon-
            do de Cultura Económica [first edition 1977].
CASO, ALFONSO, and IGNACIO BERNAL
1952   *Urnas de Oaxaca,* Memorias del Instituto Nacional de
            Antropología e Historia no. XI. Mexico City: INAH.
CASO, ALFONSO, IGNACIO BERNAL, and JORGE ACOSTA
1967   *La cerámica de Monte Albán,* Memorias del Instituto
            Nacional de Antropología e Historia no. XIII. Mexico
            City: INAH.
CHADWICK, ROBERT
1970   "The Tombs of Monte Albán I Style at Yagul," *Ancient*

MÁRQUEZ MORFÍN LOURDES, and ERNESTO GONZÁLEZ LICÓN
1992   "La trepanación craneana entre los antiguos zapotecos de Monte Albán." *Cuadernos del Sur.* 1: 25-50, May/August 1992. Oaxaca: CIESAS, INAH.

MARQUINA, IGNACIO
1990   *Arquitectura prehispánica.* Memorias del Instituto Nacional de Antropología and Historia no. I. Mexico City: INAH-SEP [facsimile of 1951 edition].

MATOS MOCTEZUMA, EDUARDO
1975   *Muerte a filo de obsidiana,* SepSetentas no. 190. Mexico City: SEP.
1990   *Teotihuacán, the City of Gods.* New York: Rizzoli International Publications, Inc.

MÉNDEZ, ENRIQUE
1990   "El descubrimiento de la Tumba 5 de Huijazóo," *Monte Albán,* Mexico City: CityCorp-CityBank.

MILLER, ARTHUR G.
1991   "The Carved Stela in Tomb 5, Suchilquitongo, Oaxaca, Mexico." *Ancient Mesoamerica* 2: 215-224.
1995   *The Painted Tombs of Oaxaca, Mexico.* Cambridge: Cambridge University Press.

MOSER, CHRISTOPHER L.
1975   "Cuerva de Ejutla: una cueva funeraria postclásica?" *Boletín del INAH* 14: 25-36.
1977   *Ñuiñe Writing and Iconography of the Mixteca Baja,* Vanderbilt University Publication in Anthropology N. 19. Nashville, Tennessee: Vanderbilt University.

NEELY, JAMES, S. C. CARAN, and B. M. WINSBOROUGH
1990   "Irrigated Agriculture at Hierve el Agua, Oaxaca, Mexico." In *Debating Oaxaca Archaeology,* edited by Joyce Marcus, 115-190. Anthropological Papers, Museum of Anthropology N. 84. Ann Arbor: University of Michigan.

NICHOLAS, LINDA M.
1989   "Land Use in Prehispanic Oaxaca." In *Monte Albán's Hinterland, Part II. Prehispanic Settlement Patterns in Tlacolula, Etla, and Ocotlan, the Valley of Oaxaca, Mexico,* edited by S. A. Kowalewski, G. M. Feinman, L. Finsten, R. E. Blanton, and L. M. Nicholas, 449-505. Memoirs of the Museum of Anthropology N. 23. Ann Arbor: University of Michigan.

NICHOLAS, LINDA M., GARY M. FEINMAN, STEPHEN A. KOWALEWSKI, RICHARD E. BLANTON, and LAURA FINSTEN
1986   "Prehispanic Colonization of the Valley of Oaxaca, Mexico," *Human Ecology* 14: 131-162.

OBREGON DE LA PARRA, JORGE
1948   "Estudio analítico de la arquitectura funeraria de Monte Albán, Oaxaca," *Actas del XXVIII Congreso Internacional de Americanistas,* Paris, 1947.

OCHOA ZAZUETA, JESÚS ANGEL
1974   *Muerte y muertos,* SepSetentas no. 153. Mexico City: SEP.

PADDOCK, JOHN (ED.)
1970   *Ancient Oaxaca.* Stanford, California: Stanford University Press.
1978   "The Middle Classic Period in Oaxaca." In *Middle Classic Mesoamerica: A.D. 400-700,* edited by Ezther Pasztory, 45-62. New York: Columbia Press University.
1983   *Lord 5 Flower's Family: Rulers of Zaachila and Cuilapan.* Publications in Anthropology N. 29. Nashville, Tennessee: Vanderbilt University.
1985   "Painted Architecture and Sculpture in Ancient Oaxaca." In *Painted Architecture and Polychrome Monumental Sculpture in Mesoamerica,* edited by Elizabeth H. Boone, 91-112. Washington, D.C.: Dumbarton Oaks Research Library and Collection.
1990   *Un milenario oaxaqueño.* Oaxaca: Casa de la Cultura Oaxaqueña.

PETERSON, DAVID ANDREWS, and THOMAS B. MacDOUGALL
1974   *Guiengola: A Fortified Site in the Isthmus of Tehuantepec.* Publications in Anthropology N. 10. Nashville, Tennessee: Vanderbilt University.

REDMON, ELSA M., and CHARLES SPENCER
1983   "The Cuicatlan Cañada and the Period II Frontier of the Zapotec State," *The Cloud People,* Kent V. Flannery and Joyce Marcus (eds.): 117-20. New York: Academic Press.

REDMON, ELSA
1984   *A Fuego y Sangre: Early Zapotec Imperialism in the Cuicatlán Cañada, Oaxaca.* Ann Arbor: Memoirs of the Museum of Anthropology, University of Michigan.

RELACIONES GEOGRÁFICAS DEL SIGLO XVI
1973   Catalogued and analyzed in *Handbook of Middle American Indians,* vol. 12, Robert Wauchope (ed.). Austin: University of Texas Press.

ROMANO, ARTURO
1974   "Sistema de enterramientos," *Antropología Física, Epoca prehispánica, México: panorama histórico y cultural,* III: 85-112. Mexico City: INAH.

ROMERO MOLINA, JAVIER
1983   "Las tumbas y los entierros prehispánicos de Oaxaca," *Anales de Antropología,* vol. XX: 91-113.

SAVILLE, MARSHALL H.
1899   "Exploration of Zapotecan Tombs in Southern Mexico," *American Anthropology* (New York) I: 350-62.
1904   "Funeral Urns from Oaxaca," *The American Museum Journal* IV: 58.
1909   "Cruciform Structures near Mitla." In *Anthropological Essays Presented to F. W. Putnam,* 151-190. New York: G. E. Stechert and Co.

SCOTT, JOHN F.
1978   "The Danzantes of Monte Albán." *Studies in Pre-Columbian Art and Archaeology,* N. 19. Washington, D.C.: Dumbarton Oaks, Trustees for Harvard University.

SEJOURNE, LAURETTE
1960   "El simbolismo de los rituales funerarios en Monte Albán," *Revista mexicana de estudios antropológicos* (Mexico City) XVI: 77-90.

SELER, EDUARD (ED.)
1896   *Die Ruinen auf dem Quie-ngola.* D. Reimer (E. Vohsen) Bastian-Festschrift. Berlin.
1901-2 *Codex Féjérváry-Mayer.* Berlin and London.
1902-3 *Codex Vaticanus* 3773. Berlin and London.
1904   "The Mexican Chronology. With special reference to the Zapotec Calendar." In *Mexican and Central American Antiquities, Calendar Systems and History.* 13-55. Washington, D.C.: Smithsonian Institution.
1963   *Códice Borgia,* 3 vols. Mexico City-Buenos Aires: Fondo de Cultura Económica.
1991   "The Ruins on Quie-ngola" [1896]. In *Collected Works in Mesoamerican Linguistics and Archaeology,* edited by J. Eric S. Thompson and F. B. Richardson, (2) 103-111. Lancaster, California: Labyrinthos.
1991   "Archaeological Results of My First Trip to Mexico" [1888]. In *Collected Works in Mesoamerican Linguistics and Archaeology,* edited by J. Eric S. Thompson and F. B. Richardson, (2) 155-202. Lancaster, California: Labyrinthos.
1993   "The Ruins of Mitla" [1906]. In *Collected Works in Mesoamerican Linguistics and Archaeology,* edited by J. Eric S. Thompson and F. B. Richardson, (4) 248-265. Lancaster, California: Labyrinthos.
1993   "Some Excellently Painted Old Pottery Vessels of the Sologuren Collection from Nochistlan and Cuicatlan in the State of Oaxaca" [1906]. In *Collected Works in Mesoamerican Linguistics and Archaeology,* edited by J. Eric S. Thompson and F. B. Richardson, (4) 285-290. Lancaster, California: Labyrinthos.

SERRA, MARI CARMEN, and YOKO SUGIURA
1977   "Las costumbres funerarias como un indicador de la estructura social en el Formativo mesoamericano," *Anales de Antropología,* vol. XIV. Mexico City: UNAM.

SPENCE, MICHAEL W.
1992   "Tlailotlacan, a Zapotec Enclave in Teotihuacan." In *Art, Ideology, and the City of Teotihuacan,* edited by J. C. Berlo, 59-88. Washington, D.C.: Dumbarton Oaks Research Library and Collection.

SPENCER, CHARLES S.
1982   *The Cuicatlán Cañada and Monte Albán. A Study of Primary State Formation.* New York: Academic Press.

SPORES, RONALD
1967   *The Mixtec Kings and Their People.* Norman, Oklahoma: University of Oklahoma Press.
1972   *An Archaeological Settlement Survey of the Nochixtlán*

Valley, Oaxaca. Vanderbilt University Publication in Anthropology N. I. Nashville, Tennessee: Vanderbilt University.

1974   "Social Stratification in Ancient Mixtec Society," *XLI International Congress of Americanists,* Mexico City.

1983   "Origins of the Village in the Mixteca (Early Cruz Phase)," *The Cloud People,* Kent V. Flannery, and Joyce Marcus (eds.). New York: Academic Press.

1984   *The Mixtecs in Ancient and Colonial Times.* Norman: University of Oklahoma Press.

STONE, DORIS

1982   "Aspects of the Mixteca-Puebla Style and Mixtec and Central Mexican Culture in Southern Mesoamerica," Papers from a Symposium organized by Doris Stone, New Orleans, *Middle American Research Institute Occasional Paper* 4.

URCID, SERRANO JAVIER

1992   Zapotec Hieroglyphic Writing. *Ph.D. Dissertation.* Yale University.

1993   "The Pacific Coast of Oaxaca and Guerrero: The Westernmost Extent of Zapotec Script." *Ancient Mesoamerica* 4: 141-165.

WHALEN, MICHAEL E.

1981   *Excavations at Santo Domingo Tomaltepec: Evolution of a Formative Community in the Valley of Oaxaca, Mexico.* Memoirs of the Museum of Anthropology N. 12. Ann Arbor: University of Michigan.

1983   "Reconstructing Early Formative Village Organization in Oaxaca, Mexico," *American Antiquity* 48: 17-43.

1988   "House and Household in Formative Oaxaca," in *Household and Community in the Mesoamerican Past*, edited by R. R. Wilk and W. Ashmore, 249-272. Albuquerque: University of New Mexico Press.

WHITECOTTON, JOSEPH W.

1977   *The Zapotecs: Princes, Priests and Peasants.* Norman: University of Oklahoma Press.

1990   *Zapotec Elite Ethnohistory: Pictorial Genealogies from Eastern Oaxaca.* Publications in Anthropology N. 39. Nashville: Vanderbilt University.

WINTER, MARCUS C.

1972   *Tierras Largas: A Formative Community in the Valley of Oaxaca, Mexico.* Ph D. dissertation. University of Arizona.

1974   "Residential Patterns at Monte Albán, Oaxaca." *Science* 186: 981-987.

ZEITLIN, ROBERT N.

1993   "Pacific Coastal Laguna Zope: A Regional Center in the Terminal Formative Hinterlands of Monte Albán," *Ancient Mesoamerica* 4: 85-101.

Illustration Credits

Color Plates

Dirección de Restauración del Patrimonio Cultural, Inah, Mexico City: 86, 87, 88, 89, 90, 91, 92, 93, 94, 95, 96, 97, 98.

Editoriale Jaca Book, Milan (photographs by Salvador Guil'liem Arroyo, Mexico City): 1, 2, 3, 4, 17, 46, 51, 52, 53, 54, 55, 56, 57, 58, 59, 60, 61, 62, 63, 64, 65, 66, 67, 68, 69, 70, 71, 72, 73, 74, 75, 76, 79, 80, 81, 82, 83, 84, 85; (photographs by Giorgio Dettori, Cagliari): 77, 78; (photographs by Antonio Maffeis and Fabio Terraneo, Tre, Milan): 5, 6, 7, 8, 9, 10, 11, 12, 13, 14, 15, 16, 18, 19, 20, 21, 22, 23, 24, 25, 26, 27, 28, 29, 30, 31, 32, 33, 34, 35, 36, 37, 38, 39, 40, 41, 42, 43, 44, 45, 47, 48, 49, 50.

Text Illustrations

Photographs

Centro Regional de Oaxaca, Inah, Oaxaca: 53, 55, 73, 80, 86, 108, 130, 133, 147, 149, 150, 151, 168.

Dirección de Restauración del Patrimonio Cultural, Inah, Mexico City: 171, 173, 174.

Editoriale Jaca Book, Milano (photographs by Salvador Guil'liem Arroyo, Mexico City): 2, 3, 4, 5, 6, 9, 14, 18, 19, 20, 21, 24, 36, 37, 48, 49, 50, 51, 52, 54, 62, 68, 74, 75, 76, 77, 78, 79, 83, 84, 85, 87, 88, 103, 119, 136, 141, 144, 145, 146, 148, 153, 154, 155, 165, 166, 167; (photographs by Giorgio Dettori, Cagliari): 134, 135, 157; (photographs by Antonio Maffeis e Fabio Terraneo, Tre, Milan): 23, 35, 44, 45, 81.

Line Drawings

Dirección de Restauración del Patrimonio Cultural, Inah, Mexico City: 10.

Editoriale Jaca Book, Milan (Daniela Balloni): 63, 64, 66, 67; (Remo Berselli): 32; (Fabio Jacomelli): 172; (Rosalba Moriggia and Maria Piatto): 1, 7, 13, 16, 22, 27, 28, 29, 31, 33, 38, 39, 40, 41, 43, 47, 56, 57, 58, 59, 60, 61, 69, 70, 71, 89, 90, 91, 92, 93, 94, 95, 96, 97, 98, 99, 100, 101, 102, 104, 105, 106, 107, 109, 110, 111, 112, 113, 114, 115, 116, 117, 118, 120, 121, 124, 125, 126, 128, 129, 131, 132, 137, 138, 140, 142, 143, 156, 158, 159, 160, 161, 163, 169, 175.

Index